YOU'RE NOT BEHIND

THE SLOW MONEY GUIDE TO MIDLIFE WEALTH AND FINANCIAL PEACE

MEL G PROSPER

frameworks are not financial advice and are for educational purposes only. Readers should consult a qualified financial adviser for personalised recommendations.

Published by The Reset Edit™

First Edition, 2025

ISBN (Print): 978-1-917926-57-7

ISBN (eBook): 978-1-917926-58-4

ISBN (Hardcover): 978-1-917926-59-1

https://www.slowmoneymovement.com/

IMPORTANT NOTE

This book is for **education and general information only**. It is not personal financial advice, investment advice, legal advice, tax advice, or therapy.

No outcome, return, or result can ever be guaranteed. All financial decisions carry risk and should be checked against your own circumstances.

Everyone's situation is different. The examples, numbers, and scenarios in this book are **illustrations**, not predictions or guarantees. Investment values can go **down as well as up**, and you may get back less than you invest.

Tax rules, allowances, and product names (such as ISAs, pensions, 401(k)s, IRAs, Social Security, and the UK State Pension) vary by country and can change over time. Always check the latest guidance for your region and, if needed, speak to a **regulated financial adviser** or qualified professional before making significant financial decisions.

The author and publisher have taken care to ensure accuracy at the time of writing, but cannot take responsibility for any losses or consequences arising from actions taken on the basis of this book. Your decisions are your own – and you deserve support that fits your life, your laws, and your nervous system.

Global Note

Throughout this book, examples may use £ or $ for simplicity. If you live elsewhere, use your local currency and equivalent systems. Retirement structures, tax rules, pensions, and financial products vary by country, but the principles in this book are universal. Always check the current rules in your region and, where appropriate, consider guidance from a properly regulated financial adviser who understands your local system.

CONTENTS

FOREWORD

Midlife doesn't announce itself.

It doesn't kick down the door or arrive with drama.

It slips in softly — almost politely — through the cracks of an ordinary day.

The quiet realisation that time isn't a limitless horizon anymore.

The gentle weight of responsibilities you never anticipated holding.

The moment the house goes still and you realise the silence feels different now.

The day you look at your life and think,

I didn't picture it happening quite like this.

I wrote this book because too many of us enter this season feeling behind, tired, and quietly ashamed of it.

We whisper things we'd never say out loud:

"I should be further ahead."

"I wasted time."

"It's too late to change anything now."

But here's a truth you haven't been told loudly enough:

You are not behind.

You are at a beginning.

Midlife isn't failure — it's awareness.

It's the moment life finally strips away the noise, the performance, the old ambitions, and leaves you face to face with what actually matters:

What brings peace?

What brings meaning?

Who am I becoming now?

This book is a hand on your shoulder.

A deep breath.

A reset button — not a stopwatch.

This isn't a sprint.

We are here to build slow, confident wealth: financial, emotional, physical.

We are here to create a life shaped by clarity rather than urgency, intention rather than exhaustion.

Time didn't run out.

It simply became more precious.

And precious things deserve care, not panic.

Across these chapters, we will move gently — from understanding where you are, to rebuilding your systems, to shaping a steadier future.

No pressure. No race. Just steady, grounded change.

If you're reading this, it means one thing:

You're ready.

Not for a dramatic reinvention — for a return.

To yourself.

To your instincts.

To a life that feels like yours again.

You haven't missed your moment — you've arrived in it.

Welcome to your reset.

— Mel G Prosper

SOFT START GUIDE

A CALMER ENTRY POINT IF YOU'RE OVERWHELMED TODAY

A Calmer Entry Point (If You're Overwhelmed Today)

A gentle beginning for the days when everything feels too much.

If life feels heavy, start here.
Small steps count — they always have.
Nothing needs to be fixed today.
Just softened.

Today

- Drink a full glass of water
- Open one account screen or bill — simply look, no action required
- Move £5/$5 into a "Future Me" pot
- Take one slow breath with a hand on your chest

One moment of presence is progress.

This Week

- Make a simple list of your accounts (rough is fine)
- Automate one tiny transfer (£5–£10)
- Replace "I'm behind" with "I'm learning"

You're not correcting the past— you're supporting the present.

This Month

- Keep one weekly ten-minute money ritual

- Choose one gentle debt or savings habit
- Rest more than you think you're "allowed" to

Your nervous system rebuilds before your numbers do.

Your Safe Reset Point

You are not late.
You are in motion.
Return to this page any time you feel overwhelmed —
it's a soft landing, a recalibration,
a place to begin again without pressure or shame.

INTRODUCTION

The Second Act Begins Quietly

Midlife rarely arrives with drama.

No crisis montage.

No sudden epiphany.

No red sports car.

It arrives quietly — a reckoning delivered through ordinary moments:

- Standing in a supermarket aisle thinking, *Is this it?*
- Feeling your stomach drop when you check a pension you haven't opened in years
- Caring for parents and teens at the same time
- Finishing work more drained than proud
- Waking at 3 a.m. worrying about money, purpose — or both
- Wondering if wanting peace makes you ungrateful

We've been sold the idea that midlife is a crisis — something chaotic, loud, dramatic.

But the truth is simpler:

Midlife is a turning point that whispers before it shifts.

It's the soft, stubborn knowing that rises inside you:

I want a life that feels like mine again.

Not a performance.

Not an endurance test.

Not a calendar full of obligations.

A life lived on purpose — not by momentum.

And yes — money plays a role.

Not because money is the goal, but because money creates:

• options

• breathing room

• dignity

• calm

This isn't a book about hustling out of stress.

It's not about catching up with anyone else's timeline.

It's not about racing strangers on the internet.

It's about rebuilding a financial life that supports the person you've become —

not the identity you outgrew.

You're here because something in you wants:

Peace more than urgency.

Meaning more than applause.

Security more than spectacle.

A more grounded way to live.

You don't need a sprint.

You need a return.

If your brain, health, energy, or capacity works differently — because of neurodiversity, illness, burnout, caregiving, or life circumstances — this approach is designed to flex, not demand perfection.

How to Read This Book

Take this slowly.

Let it settle.

Move one chapter, one idea, one gentle step at a time.

There are three parts to this journey:

Part I — Reset Mindset

Where we soften shame, dismantle old stories, and rebuild self-trust.

Part II — Rebuild Systems

Where money becomes calmer through simple, sustainable structures.

Part III — Renew Life

Where work, energy, boundaries, and future plans align with who you are now.

You are not expected to implement everything at once.

You're not even expected to feel ready.

You only need willingness — the smallest amount — to begin again.

This isn't a sprint.

It's a homecoming.

By reading these words, you've already started your reset.

Awareness is movement.

Curiosity is movement.

Turning toward your financial life with gentleness is movement.

In the next chapter, we meet you exactly where you are —
not with judgement, but with clarity.

Let's begin.

PART I — RESET MINDSET

"SLOW IS STRONG."

CHAPTER 1
WHERE YOU ARE NOW
YOUR MIDLIFE MONEY STARTING POINT

Midlife rarely arrives with a clear moment.

There's no milestone balloon, no congratulatory announcement, no cinematic crescendo.

Instead, it shows up quietly — through the small, honest moments you almost overlook:

A late-night Google search about retirement projections.

A Google search that starts with 'how much do I need to retire' and ends with 'midlife memes'.

A pension login you can't remember because you haven't checked it in far too long.

A sigh when the credit card bill lands — again.

A strange mix of pride and ache when your child becomes more independent.

A pause when a parent repeats the same question twice, and you realise roles have shifted.

A morning when you wake up more tired than when you went to bed.

There's no single alarm bell that announces this season.

It builds — thought by thought, responsibility by responsibility.

And then one day, you catch yourself thinking:

Is this where I thought I'd be?

And if not… what now?

This book meets you in that exact place —
in the pause,
in the quiet reckoning,
in the tender, sacred in-between where change begins.

In this chapter, we begin with honesty. In the chapters ahead, you'll build stability, clarity, systems, and a sustainable pace — but it starts here.

THE FEELING NOBODY TALKS ABOUT

People imagine midlife sounds like:

"Crisis."

"Meltdown."

"Panic."

But truly, midlife often sounds like this:

"I'm tired in a way sleep doesn't fix."

"I want peace, not pressure."

"Something in me is shifting." And somewhere beneath all of this, your financial life is shifting too — not just the numbers, but the meaning behind them.

"I don't need more — I need enough."

"I didn't come this far to feel like this."

And then the quiet sentence — the one that arrives not as a scream, but as a whisper:

I want my life to feel like mine again.

Not reactive.

Not rushed.

Not lived in permanent survival mode.

Not performed like you're still keeping up with a script someone else wrote.

Just lived.

Owned.

Chosen.

. . .

Most midlifers don't need a new budget — they need a new starting point.

You Expected Certainty — and Got Questions

When we were younger, midlife looked like the promised land.

People in their 40s and 50s seemed steady.

Certain.

Sorted.

They had homes, pensions, routines.

They looked like they knew who they were.

Now that you're here?

You realise most adults are walking, breathing contradictions:

- Exhausted and ambitious
- Grateful and restless
- Proud and disappointed
- Capable and overwhelmed
- Wise — yet still unsure
- Wishing for stability while craving change

You don't lack clarity because you're lost.

You lack clarity because you've evolved —
and the life you built hasn't fully caught up with who you've become.

That's not failure.

That's truth rising.

Growth in your 20s is about building a life.

Growth in your 40s and 50s is about refining one.

Letting go of noise.

Reclaiming energy.

Choosing with intention, not autopilot.

Midlife isn't the end of knowing who you are —
it's the beginning of knowing yourself deeply.

WHY THIS MOMENT MATTERS

There's a myth that transformation belongs to the young.

That growth is something you do early — while you still have time to "figure things out."

That's nonsense.

Midlife change is different.

Not louder.

Deeper.

It's not about proving yourself anymore.

It's about *knowing* yourself.

Choosing with intention instead of momentum.

This isn't a crisis.

It's a calling — a shift toward a life that finally aligns with your values, your boundaries, and your truth.

You are not starting over.

You are starting *from experience.*

And that changes everything.

Pause. Acknowledge Yourself.

Before we talk about numbers, tools, or strategy, pause for a moment and notice what you've already carried:

You have supported people.

You've held things together when life stretched thin.

You've made decisions without a manual.

You've adapted, adjusted, survived storms, and kept moving.

You have resilience earned through experience — not optimism.

Knowledge gathered from life — not textbooks.

Even if you're tired, you're still standing.

And standing in midlife is not a small thing.

It means:

Life knocked.

You answered.

You stayed.

Let yourself register that.

You're not weak.

You're weathered and wise — and that is a different kind of strength.

The Secret Everyone Carries Here

There's a quiet contradiction almost everyone feels in midlife:

We feel behind —

while doing more than we ever have.

You might recognise yourself in one or more of these:

- You've built stability, but feel fragile beneath it.
- You've worked for decades, yet feel money hasn't worked for you.
- You give to children, parents, relationships, work — and keep the leftovers for yourself.
- You're grateful, but rarely rested.
- You're accomplished, but quietly anxious about the future.
- You've lived a full life, yet still feel there's more in you.

This isn't weakness.

This is transition — the shift from:

"What can I do for everyone else?"

to

"What do I want the rest of my life to feel like?"

That's not a breakdown.

It's an awakening.

You are not alone in this.

You are not unusual.

You are not behind.

The Money Truth of Midlife

Let's name the reality gently and clearly:

Midlife money isn't just numbers.

It's identity.

It's self-trust.

It's security and dignity.

It's the voice at 3am whispering,

"Will I be okay?"

You may be financially responsible —

and emotionally tired from carrying that responsibility alone.

You may have income —

and also commitments that stretch further than they used to.

You may have had years to save —

and still feel like real life interrupted the spreadsheet more often than not.

You might have a pension —

but it feels foggy and unnervingly small.

You may have been sensible —

and still feel a single life event away from wobbling.

This isn't because you "failed at money."

It's because:

Most of us were never taught financial ease —

only financial urgency.

And midlife finances often look like this:

- A mortgage or rent that still bites.
- Kids who need support — or return unexpectedly.
- Parents who quietly rely on you.
- Long work hours but less emotional payoff.
- Savings that don't reflect how hard you've worked.
- Retirement accounts that feel abstract and distant.
- Inflation nibbling at every corner of your budget.
- A nervous system that refuses hustle culture.
- A growing desire for slower mornings and more meaningful work.

And beneath it all?

A quiet fear:

"Did I miss my chance?"

You didn't.

You're simply at the doorway where money needs to shift from aggression to intention.

From pressure to clarity.

From fear to steadiness.

Midlife money isn't about "more."
It's about *calmer, wiser*.

The Emotional Cost of Carrying So Much

Money at midlife isn't just about accounts or spreadsheets — it's about who you've had to be.

It's about identity.
Self-trust.
Security.
Legacy.
Freedom.
Worth.
It's the 3am voice that whispers:
"Will I be okay?"
It's filling out a form asking "retirement goal" and wanting to write only one word:
peace.

You are not weak for feeling stretched.

You are stretched because you've carried so much — often quietly, often alone.

You may have been the one who held everything together.
The one who remembered every detail.
The one who adapted when life changed shape.
The one who kept showing up, even when you were exhausted.
That isn't failure.
That's endurance with a heartbeat.

And endurance comes with a cost — a quiet fatigue that builds across years, not days.

This chapter is your permission slip to finally say:
"I am tired because I have done a lot. I deserve systems, not strain."

A Story: Anna & David

Meet Anna, 52.
Widowed at 49.
A mortgage on her shoulders.
A pension she's scared to open.
Adult children who assume she's "fine."
She isn't "fine."
She's functioning.
Working, paying bills, smiling when she must —
yet feeling vulnerable in a way she never expected.
She doesn't want inspiration.
She wants stability.
She wants calm.

Now meet David, 47.
Divorced.
Two teenagers.
A career shaken by restructuring.
Debt he never expected to carry again.
He used to feel competent with money.
Now he hesitates to check his balance.
Not irresponsible — just exhausted.
Both believe everyone their age is doing better.
Both are wrong.
Both are normal.
And both are capable of rebuilding — not through frantic hustle,
but through **patient direction**.

That's what this book gives you:
The shift from fearful reacting → to calm creating.

THE MIDLIFE MIND SHIFT: FROM JUDGEMENT TO LEADERSHIP

Ask yourself gently:

Have you been judging where you are…
or leading from where you are?

Most of us have been judging.
Judgement paralyses.
Leadership empowers.
Judgement says:
"You should have known better."
"You're too late."
"You messed up."
"You should be further ahead."
Leadership says:
"Okay. I'm here. What matters now? Let's take one step."
Feel the difference in your body?
One contracts.
One expands.
This book teaches you to lead your second act —
not apologise for your first one.

THE GENTLE AUDIT

Before we move into strategy, let's do what most financial books skip:

Not numbers.
Not budgets.
A **self-state check**.
Grab a page — or open your notes app.
Title it:
Where I Truly Am
Then answer these slowly, without overthinking:

- Emotionally, right now I feel…
- Financially, I often feel…
- What I wish people understood about me is…
- What I'm most proud of is…
- What scares me most financially is…
- What I secretly hope for next is…
- If nothing changed for five years, I would feel…
- I want to feel more…
- I want to feel less…
- One thing I no longer want to carry into the second act is…
- One thing I absolutely want to create is…

You've just begun your financial reset — internally first.

We never start with spreadsheets.

We start with honesty and gentleness, because money follows mindset, not the other way around.

A Declaration for Your Second Act

This isn't about strategy yet.

It's about identity.

Say this quietly, or write it down:

"I am allowed to reset.

I am allowed to start again.

I am not behind — I am evolving."

If you take only one message from this chapter, let it be this:

You are not late.

You are ready.

And readiness in midlife is far more powerful than confidence in youth.

Confidence comes from innocence.

Midlife action comes from truth.

Truth is stronger.

THREE SLOW-MONEY RITUALS FOR YOUR FIRST STEPS

These rituals are not tasks.

They're grounding practices — a way to bring your nervous system into the conversation.

1. The Morning Naming

Each morning this week, speak one quiet truth aloud:

"I am learning."

"I am allowed to start again."

"I don't have to rush to build something strong."

"I am capable."

"I am building a calm future."

• • •

Pick one. Repeat it.
Not hype — permission.

2. The Five-Minute Financial Presence
Not planning.
Not fixing.
Just *looking*.
Spend five minutes this week:
• Open your banking app
• Glance at your pension
• Look at your accounts
• Read a savings balance
Notice without judgement.
We don't change what we fear.
We change what we can sit with.
Presence comes before progress.

3. The Midlife Compass
Write a sentence beginning with:
"In the next chapter of my life, I want..."
Let it end honestly:
"...peace more than prestige."
"...time more than applause."
"...steady growth, not frantic beginnings."
"...a financial life that feels like exhaling, not bracing."
Put your sentence where you'll see it.
This reset isn't about catching up —
it's about reorienting.

What You Just Did

You didn't prepare to begin.
You already began.
Awareness + compassion = agency.
You didn't buy a new identity.

You returned to the one that was waiting for you.

KEY TAKEAWAYS

• You're not behind — you're arriving.

• Your financial story makes sense once you honour your lived reality.

• Shame lifts when truth is allowed to breathe.

Tiny Action:

□ Write one honest sentence beginning with:
"Right now, my financial life feels like…"

In this chapter, you met yourself honestly — without judgement.
That is the foundation for everything that follows.
Next, we dismantle the most stubborn midlife belief:
"It's too late."
Spoiler:
The data, the lived examples, and your own instincts say otherwise.
You are arriving — not ending.

"I BUILD WEALTH AT THE PACE OF MY NERVOUS SYSTEM."

CHAPTER 2
THE MYTH OF "TOO LATE"
WHY YOU ARE RIGHT ON TIME

The belief that you're "too late" doesn't arrive because you failed.

It arrives because you finally paused long enough to see your life clearly.

Midlife exposes truth — quietly, but undeniably.

You notice the pension that didn't grow the way you hoped.

The savings pot that never had a chance to recover from real life.

The mortgage that still sits on your shoulders.

The responsibilities that expanded while your time and energy shrank.

The years that blurred together through work, caregiving, crises, and sheer endurance.

You're not starting from zero.

You're just finally aware.

And awareness can feel like panic when you're exhausted.

This belief — *"I've missed my chance"* — isn't a character flaw.

It's a perfectly human response to:

- Emotional fatigue
- Caring for everyone else first
- Constant comparison (especially online)
- Life interruptions that derailed the neat plans you once had
- A body and mind that no longer tolerate chaos

- The cultural myth that midlife should be "sorted"
- The quiet grief of time passing

You expected this season to bring certainty.

Instead, it brought questions.

No wonder your brain spins the story:

"It's too late."

But here's the grounded truth:

It's not too late.

It's simply *later than you expected* — and that is not the same thing.

You're arriving at this moment with more clarity, more wisdom, more resilience, and more self-awareness than you've ever had before.

This isn't the end of possibility.

It's the beginning of **intentional possibility** — the kind built on truth, not fantasy.

In midlife, "too late" is rarely fact.

It's a feeling.

And feelings are not the same as reality.

WHAT "BEHIND" REALLY MEANS — THE PSYCHOLOGICAL TRAP

Feeling "behind" is not an accurate assessment of your life.

It's a psychological miscalculation — a gap between expectation and reality that widens in midlife.

Here's why:

1. You're comparing yourself to a version of you that never existed.

You expected uninterrupted years of steady saving, clear career progression, calm health, stable relationships, and predictable life events.

But real life… interrupts.

Illness.

Divorce.

Redundancy.

Children.

Parents.

Unexpected costs.

A global pandemic.

Exhaustion.

Grief.

You didn't fall behind.

Life happened.

And let's be honest — half of midlife is just Googling 'why am I tired?' and getting wildly unhelpful answers.

2. Midlife increases awareness but decreases energy.

You finally see the full picture — your money, choices, patterns — with sharp clarity.

But awareness arrives at the exact moment your nervous system says, "I can't do chaos anymore."

The mismatch? Normal.

3. You're comparing your inside to everyone else's outside.

People your age don't post their overdrafts, arguments, pension gaps, debt, fear, or regret.

They post holidays, home renovations, promotions, new kitchens, smiling family photos.

You're comparing your reality to someone else's highlight reel.

It's not a fair measurement.

4. You inherited a timeline that never served you.

Society taught us:

"Sorted by 30."

"Established by 40."

"Coasting by 50."

Completely unrealistic timelines built for a world that no longer exists.

Midlife today is not midlife in 1985.

The economy changed.

The housing market changed.
Work changed.
Family life changed.
Retirement ages changed.
But the expectations stayed the same.
You're not behind.
You're living in a different era with outdated cultural scripts.

5. "Behind" is a feeling — not a fact.

When you're tired, overwhelmed, or carrying too much, your brain defaults to self-blame.

It's easier to say, "I should be further ahead,"
than to acknowledge:
"I've carried more than most people will ever understand."
Feeling behind means you care.
Feeling behind means you're aware.
Feeling behind means you're ready.
Awareness is movement — even when it feels like fear.

Micro-Story: Mya, 47

Mya sat in her car outside the pharmacy, looking at her bank app again, heart pounding even though the numbers hadn't changed.

She whispered, "How did everyone else figure this out?"

But when she finally opened her notebook and wrote her numbers down, something surprising happened — her panic softened.

Nothing had changed except her clarity, yet that alone shifted the weight.

Your journey will feel like this too — not dramatic, just steadier.

Where We Go Next

Now that we've dismantled the emotional story,
the next section gives you something stronger:
the data.
Data removes panic.
Data removes shame.

Data shows the truth: most midlife money beliefs are based on assumption, not reality.

And reality is far kinder than your fear.

THE DATA THAT DEBUNKS MIDLIFE FINANCIAL PANIC

Here's the truth the fear never tells you:

Most people build the majority of their wealth in their 40s, 50s, and early 60s — not their 20s or 30s. (Based on median net worth data from UK ONS and widely cited financial research.)

This isn't an opinion.

It's how human financial lives actually play out.

Let's break it down gently.

1. Your highest-earning years are usually midlife.

Most people reach peak earnings between 45–60.

Not 25.

Not 30.

That means your strongest financial years are ahead, not behind.

2. Retirement savings often spike later — not earlier.

Many people contribute little in their 20s and 30s due to:

- low wages
- childcare
- rent/mortgages
- debt
- survival mode

But contributions jump dramatically once children grow, careers stabilise, and income rises.

It's normal for pension pots to look unimpressive until midlife — then grow quickly.

3. Compound growth accelerates later too.

The early years feel slow.

The later years feel fast.

Why?

Because compounding amplifies bigger contributions.

Yes, compounding favours time — but size matters too.

Smaller contributions in your twenties grow… but a meaningful contribution in your forties can *still* outgrow them.

You're not late. You're just starting with more power. Late starts are not failures.

They're mathematically effective.

Important: *None of this is a promise or prediction. Markets move, life shifts, and no strategy can remove risk. What this does mean is that* ***starting now, with steady contributions and a clear plan, still has real power*** *— even if you began later than you were told you "should."*

4. Career pivots peak in midlife — and often increase income.

People aged 40–55 are now one of the largest groups changing careers, upgrading skills, launching small businesses, or moving into better-paid roles.

Second-act careers are often more aligned — and better paid.

5. Debt payoff tends to happen later — and frees up huge cashflow.

Many people clear mortgages, car loans, or old debts in midlife.

Once that happens, hundreds of pounds a month become available for:

- pensions
- savings
- investments
- emergency funds
- lifestyle upgrades
- reduced stress

Midlife cashflow is powerful.

• • •

6. Life expectancy has extended — so your "window" is larger than you were taught.

You're not running out of time.

You're adjusting to a longer runway.

There is space.

There is time.

There is potential.

Why This Matters More Than You Think

Most midlifers have never been told the truth:

you weren't supposed to feel "set for life" in your twenties or thirties.

Those decades give you experience — not stability.

Midlife isn't late.

Midlife is when financial lives *naturally* consolidate, compound, and clarify.

And when the shame drops — even a little — your capacity rises.

Not because you suddenly "try harder,"

but because your nervous system finally has space to breathe.

A Quiet Example

Take Sara, 49.

She spent most of her thirties overwhelmed and most of her forties catching up.

Last year she started investing for the first time with £150 a month.

A colleague of hers began in their twenties — but stopped, started, panicked, withdrew, restarted, and repeated the cycle for two decades.

Today?

Sara is projected to surpass them within eight years.

Not because she started earlier — but because she started *steadier*.

This is what the myth of "too late" never tells you:

aligned action compounds faster than frantic action.

The Data Speaks Clearly: You're Not Late — You're Right On Schedule

If your financial life feels like a late spring instead of a bright summer, that's normal.

Most midlife financial stories **start blooming now** — quietly at first, then unmistakably.

You're not behind.

You're entering the years where clarity, capability, and compounding finally align.

Next, We Shift the Lens

You've seen the emotional story.

You've seen the real-world data.

Now we're going to reshape the belief itself —

to give you a new definition of timing that matches the life you're building now.

THE SLOW MONEY REFRAME — THE TRUTH ABOUT TIMING

Timing isn't about age.

It's about awareness.

You can only build the life you want from the version of you that finally understands what matters.

Midlife gives you that understanding.

You're not starting late.

You're starting *from clarity*.

And clarity is more powerful than time.

Think of everything you didn't know in your twenties and thirties — about money, boundaries, relationships, work, your own capacity, your values, your nervous system, your limits, your worth.

Why would you want your financial story written by the least experienced version of you?

This is the season where your decisions carry weight because **you** now carry wisdom.

That's not lateness.

That's precision.

A New Definition of Timing

Slow Money timing sounds like this:

"Now that I know myself, I can finally build for myself."

or

"I begin when I'm ready — and I'm ready now."

or

"The right time is the moment I stop pretending I'm behind."

Slow Money doesn't follow cultural timelines.

It follows *self-honesty*.

And self-honesty arrives in midlife like a new compass — quiet, steady, reliable.

You Are Arriving — Not Catching Up

Here is the grounded truth the fear never tells you:

Midlife isn't the end of possibility—it's the end of self-doubt disguised as possibility.

You're not catching up.

You're stepping in.

Into your voice.

Into your clarity.

Into your second act.

Into the financial future that finally feels like it belongs to you.

And that is the perfect moment to begin.

KEY TAKEAWAYS

- "Too late" is a cultural illusion, not a personal truth.
- Midlife is a powerful, strategic beginning.
- Your timing is not a flaw — it's context.

Tiny Action

□ Write one honest sentence beginning with:

"If I wasn't late, I would..."

You don't need to act on it.

Just let the truth surface.

. . .

You've dismantled the myth.

You've understood the psychology.

You've seen the data.

Now you're ready for the next shift:

Your identity.

In Chapter 3, we explore who you are becoming —

and how self-trust, not urgency, becomes the foundation for the wealth you'll build next.

Your future isn't shrinking.

It's opening.

Where We're Going Next

If the myth of "too late" kept you frozen,

the truth about your midlife strengths will set you free.

In the next chapter, we step into the real power of this season —

the awakening you've been sensing but couldn't yet name.

“SMALL STEPS COMPOUND INTO BIG CHANGE.”

CHAPTER 3

THE MIDLIFE AWAKENING – SEEING YOUR FINANCIAL LIFE CLEARLY

THE QUIET SHIFT INSIDE YOU

Midlife doesn't change you in one dramatic moment.

There's no grand announcement.

No sudden reinvention.

No cinematic transformation.

Instead, something inside you begins to stir — quietly, steadily, persistently.

You notice it in small ways:

The book you used to devour now feels shallow.

The goals that once energised you now feel strangely flat.

The job you tolerated for years suddenly feels too tight around the edges.

The conversations you used to accept now drain you.

The habits you clung to out of loyalty no longer make sense.

The noise you once ignored now feels unbearable.

Nothing is "wrong."

You're simply becoming more *you*.

This is the midlife awakening — not a crisis, but a calibration.

A subtle shift from:

"Who should I be?"

to

"Who am I, truly?"

And once this shift begins, it's impossible to un-notice.

Your values sharpen.

Your tolerance for nonsense dissolves.

Your desire for meaning strengthens.

Your awareness deepens.

Your honesty with yourself becomes sharper and kinder at the same time.

It's not a breakdown.

It's a breakthrough that whispers.

A quiet inner voice saying:

This life was good, but now I want it to fit me better.

A life that feels aligned.

A life that feels steady.

A life that finally feels like home.

That's the awakening.

Not the chaos — the clarity.

And clarity always asks for a response.

And when clarity rises, it often meets friction — because the old version of you still thinks it's in charge.

IDENTITY BURNOUT — THE HIDDEN WEIGHT OF MIDLIFE

Identity burnout happens when the version of you that carried you through your 20s, 30s, and early 40s has simply run out of road.

You've outgrown the old operating system —

but you haven't yet stepped fully into the new one.

It's the moment you feel:

- tired of pretending you're fine
- disconnected from goals you once cared about
- overstretched by responsibilities that no longer feel aligned
- less patient with chaos
- more aware of what drains you
- confused about why you're not satisfied
- quietly longing for a different way of living

. . .

This isn't depression.

It's not failure.

It's not a personality flaw.

It's the natural consequence of living many chapters without stopping to ask,

"Do these choices still fit me?"

The person you were 10 or 15 years ago built a life based on:

- ambition
- survival
- approval
- necessity
- momentum
- 'shoulds'
- other people's needs
- old dreams

That version of you was doing their best.

And they did well.

But now...

you're different.

Your values changed.

Your limits changed.

Your body changed.

Your priorities changed.

Your tolerance changed.

Your internal compass finally has a signal strong enough to follow.

And the life built by your *previous self* no longer matches your *current self.*

That mismatch is identity burnout.

A Quiet Story From Real Life

A woman I worked with told me she woke up one morning in her late forties and felt an unexpected heaviness — not depression, not crisis, just a quiet sense that the life she'd built no longer fit the person she'd become.

She said, "Nothing is wrong… and yet everything feels slightly misaligned."

She wasn't falling apart.

She was **outgrowing** the version of herself who survived her twenties, proved herself in her thirties, and carried everyone through her forties.

This wasn't a breakdown.

It was the beginning of recognition —

the moment she realised her identity needed recalibrating, not rescuing.

Outgrowing Old Versions of You

You're not lost.

You're shedding.

Outgrowing the you who said yes to too much.

Outgrowing the you who didn't know how to rest.

Outgrowing the you who tolerated things that hurt you.

Outgrowing the you who based decisions on fear or scarcity.

Outgrowing the you who kept the peace at your own expense.

Outgrowing the you who didn't yet understand your own worth.

Outgrowing the you who pushed through everything.

Midlife isn't asking you to throw your life away.

It's asking you to update it.

To choose with clarity instead of obligation.

To build with intention instead of autopilot.

To finally inhabit the life you've earned, not the one you inherited.

This isn't identity loss.

It's identity precision.

The beginning of living as the person you've quietly been becoming.

Identity affects money more than motivation ever will.

Because every financial system you build will only work as well as the self-trust underneath it.

Where We Go Next

Identity shifts aren't just emotional —
they're physiological.
Your body begins to refuse chaos.
Your nervous system becomes your truth-teller.
And that's where we go next:

why your body is demanding a calmer financial life, and why that's not weakness — it's wisdom.

THE NERVOUS SYSTEM RESET — WHY YOUR BODY REFUSES CHAOS NOW

Something shifts in your body in midlife — something important, intelligent, and often misunderstood.
You're not "less motivated."
You're not "losing your edge."
You're not "getting too old for stress."
Your nervous system is recalibrating.

Regulation simply means your body has enough capacity to take in information without panic, fog, or shutdown. It doesn't require feeling calm — it just means you feel steady enough to choose, respond, and think. A regulated nervous system gives you space to look at numbers, consider options, and stay present with reality instead of reacting to it.

Dysregulation is different. It's when your body flips into fight, flight, freeze, or fawn. Dysregulation feels like urgency, avoidance, irritability, fogginess, catastrophising, compulsive action, or complete shutdown. It isn't a moral failing — it's biology. Your body isn't being dramatic. It's trying to keep you safe with the tools it learned years ago.

• • •

When you understand this, money stops feeling like a threat and starts feeling like something you can relate to with steadiness and clarity.

Nothing in this chapter replaces therapy, medication, or professional mental health support. If you're living with trauma, burnout, or ongoing anxiety or depression, you deserve ***more than a book*** *— you deserve proper care. The tools here are designed to work* ***alongside*** *support, not in place of it.*

When you were younger, you could push through almost anything:
late nights, emotional chaos, financial uncertainty, drama, noise, constant change.
Your nervous system absorbed it all —
not because it was healthy,
but because it was adaptable.
Midlife changes that.

Financial freeze is one of the most misunderstood nervous-system responses. It looks like procrastination, but it's actually protection. You avoid opening letters, avoid checking balances, avoid making decisions — not because you don't care, but because your system feels overloaded. Freeze happens when the task feels bigger than the capacity you have left. Naming it removes shame, and once shame dissolves, clarity can finally begin.

Here's what actually happens:

1. Your stress tolerance becomes more honest.
You can no longer ignore the emotional cost of things.
Your body tells the truth faster than your mind can justify it.

2. You reject chaos instinctively.
Not out of weakness,
but because chaos inhibits clarity —
and clarity is now your priority.

3. You need stability to think clearly.
Uncertainty drains more energy now.
Your decisions require grounding, not turbulence.

4. Your body chooses longevity over adrenaline.
The rush you once lived on?
Now it feels like depletion, not excitement.

5. You recognise emotional safety as a financial need.
An unstable nervous system makes reactive money decisions.
A regulated one builds long-term wealth.

6. You feel the cost of stress in real time.
Your body speaks up sooner:
tight chest, foggy thinking, shallow breathing, irritability, fatigue.
This isn't decline.
This is wisdom.
Your body is not shutting down —
it's narrowing the gap between what you tolerate and what you truly need.
It's not asking for a smaller life.
It's asking for a steadier one.

And that steadiness is the foundation of Slow Money.

Because sustainable wealth isn't built from urgency.

It's built from regulated clarity.

When your nervous system is calm, you make different choices:

- cleaner choices
- long-term choices
- self-respecting choices
- boundary-led choices
- clear-eyed choices
- confident choices

This shift isn't a setback.
It's a redesign.
Your body is quietly saying:
"I want the second act to be lived, not survived."
And that changes how you work, spend, save, invest, and plan.

Where We Go Next

Now that you understand the shift happening inside you — emotionally and physiologically —

we end the chapter with the most important part:

who you're becoming.

Your identity is recalibrating,
your body is guiding you differently,
and your values are sharper than ever.

The next section ties all of this into a powerful identity declaration — the one that carries you into the rest of the book.

Who You're Becoming Now

You are not becoming someone new.

You're finally becoming someone honest.

The pressure-led version of you — the one who pushed, tolerated, absorbed, and endured — did what they needed to do to survive earlier chapters of life.

But that's not the version leading your second act.

Here's who is emerging:

1. Someone who chooses meaning over momentum
You no longer chase what doesn't align.
You choose what feels true.

2. Someone who notices your own limits
You recognise them not as weaknesses,
but as boundaries — the edges that protect you.

3. Someone with emotional clarity
You sense misalignment faster.
You filter noise quicker.
You listen to yourself more easily.

4. Someone who wants calm, not adrenaline
Not because you're "slowing down,"
but because you've outgrown chaos.

5. Someone who values time differently
It's no longer something to squeeze.
It's something to honour.

6. Someone willing to build steadiness
Not perfection.
Not performance.
Just steadiness.

7. Someone who knows the cost of self-abandonment
And refuses to pay it again.

8. Someone ready for a financial life that protects you — not depletes you
A life built on intention, not survival.
This is the person who will build the wealth, peace, stability, and clarity of your second act.
This is the person capable of slow, sustainable, confident change.
You are not "reinventing" yourself.
You are returning to the version of you that your earlier self never had the space to become.

YOUR IDENTITY DECLARATION FOR THE SECOND ACT

Say this gently — or write it down:

> **"I am no longer surviving my life.**
> **I am shaping it."**
> And if you feel it, add:
> **"I am ready to build something that honours who I am now."**

Identity first.
Strategy second.
This is the Slow Money way.

KEY TAKEAWAYS

- Identity shifts create financial shifts.
- You cannot build Act Two with Act One's identity.
- Self-trust begins by meeting yourself honestly.

Tiny Action

□ Write one sentence beginning with:
"What part of me am I outgrowing?"

You've met the real you —
the you underneath all the roles, stresses, and expectations.
The you who wants a calmer, more intentional financial life.
The you who makes decisions from clarity, not chaos.
The you who is becoming the author of your second act.
Next, we build the foundation that this new identity needs:
self-trust.

Because no plan — no matter how brilliant — works without the one thing your first act never taught you:

How to trust yourself with money.

That's where Chapter 4 begins.

"CONSISTENCY IS LOUDER THAN INTENSITY."

CHAPTER 4
SLOW MONEY FOUNDATIONS – BUILDING A CALM FINANCIAL BASE

THE PHILOSOPHY OF SLOW MONEY — WHY THIS APPROACH WORKS IN MIDLIFE

Slow Money isn't about taking your foot off the gas.

It's about putting your energy where it actually creates results — steadily, calmly, and in a way your life can hold.

By midlife, you've learned something younger versions of you couldn't see:

Intensity burns out fast.

Urgency creates mistakes.

Overhauls rarely last.

What you need now is steadiness — not speed.

Slow Money is built for the reality of your life today:

- your responsibilities
- your energy
- your nervous system
- your bandwidth
- your limits
- your values
- your desires
- your future

Not the fantasy version of life that traditional finance assumes.

Traditional advice tells you to:

- cut harder
- hustle more
- work longer
- sacrifice everything now for later
- fix everything immediately

That advice was written for people with limitless energy, limitless time, and no one depending on them.

Not you.

Slow Money recognises the truth:

You're not starting from scratch.

You're starting from experience.

And experience needs a different kind of plan — one that respects your season, your health, your pace, and your actual life.

Slow Money replaces:

overwhelm → with rhythm

panic → with clarity

shame → with self-respect

chaos → with structure

urgency → with intention

It doesn't demand pressure.

It creates capacity.

Slow Money works in midlife because it doesn't ask you to become someone else.

It works with the person you are now — wise, stretched, discerning, and ready for something real.

Something sustainable.

Something you can live with.

Something that genuinely feels like you.

Take a breath before we go deeper — this next part isn't criticism of you.

It's a breakdown of why the system was never built for your life.

Example:

Think of Aisha, 47. For years, she tried to "fix" her money by jumping straight into investing and side hustles, but every small setback sent her spiralling. When we mapped her situation, we realised she didn't have a real floor: no emergency fund, no clear view of her monthly numbers, and no protection if she got sick. Once she built a tiny £500 buffer, simplified her accounts, and put basic insurance in place, something shifted. She didn't feel "rich" — she felt held. That's the power of foundations.

WHY TRADITIONAL BUDGETING FAILS MIDLIFERS

This next part isn't about failure — it's about fit.

A Real Midlife Moment

A reader once told me she tried a colour-coded budget every January for six years.

By week three, life had already thrown three curveballs — a shift change, a sick child, and an unexpected bill — and the whole system collapsed.

She wasn't undisciplined.

Her life was simply real.

Traditional budgeting wasn't built for you.

It was built for people with:

- simple lives
- predictable routines
- minimal responsibilities
- unlimited evenings and weekends
- linear careers
- stable health
- no dependants

• • •

In other words:

people who do not exist in midlife.

Midlife money isn't neat.

It's layered with:

- children
- parents
- mortgages
- health shifts
- career shifts
- fatigue
- inflation
- loss
- caregiving
- unexpected bills
- emotional load
- the invisible weight of holding everyone else together

A spreadsheet can't hold all of that.

And yet, traditional budgeting assumes:

"Just track everything."

"Just be disciplined."

"Just say no to treats."

"Just try harder."

If "trying harder" worked, it would've worked by now.

Midlife isn't about trying harder.

It's about planning smarter — in a way your **nervous system can actually hold**.

Here's why traditional budgeting collapses in midlife:

1. It ignores decision fatigue.

You're not dealing with one budget.

You're dealing with 100 micro-decisions a day.

Every "should I…?" drains your energy.

A complicated budget adds more decisions — not fewer.

Slow Money removes decision fatigue by creating **autopilot structure**, not endless tracking.

. . .

2. It assumes you can willpower your way through everything.

Willpower is a fragile resource in midlife.

Responsibilities drain it long before money tasks begin.

You don't need more discipline.

You need fewer triggers.

3. It ignores emotional load.

Traditional budgeting pretends:

money = maths

But in midlife:

money = responsibility

money = safety

money = exhaustion

money = identity

money = fear

money = hope

money = pressure

money = survival stories

Traditional budgeting gives you a spreadsheet.

Slow Money gives you space.

4. It collapses the moment life gets loud.

A sick parent.

A stressful month at work.

A school bill.

A car repair.

A flare-up of old stress or burnout.

Traditional budgets break the second your life becomes real.

Slow Money expects interruptions — and builds flexibility in from the start.

5. It's built on guilt.

Traditional budgeting is basically:

"You overspent."
"You failed."
"You should've known better."
"Do it perfectly next month."
Shame isn't a strategy.
It's paralysis.
Slow Money is built on **returning**, not perfection.

6. It has no respect for your nervous system.

If a budgeting system spikes your cortisol, you will avoid it.
Not because you're irresponsible —
because your body is trying to protect you.
Your financial plan has to regulate your nervous system, not activate it.
Slow Money does exactly that.

7. It doesn't account for midlife identity change.

You are not the same person you were ten years ago.
You don't want the same life.
You don't have the same bandwidth.
You don't tolerate the same chaos.
You don't believe the same things.
A budget built for your past self cannot serve your present self.

The Truth

Traditional budgeting fails midlifers
not because you're bad with money
but because the rules were never written for your life.
Slow Money gives you a different model —
one that works with your energy, your responsibilities, your season, your reality.
Next, we lay out the core principles
that make midlife rebuilding sustainable, steady, and human.

THE SLOW MONEY PRINCIPLES

Slow Money isn't about doing less.

It's about doing what works — steadily, calmly, and without the panic cycles that drained you in the past.

These principles are your emotional anchors and your practical compass.

They're simple on purpose.

Your nervous system can hold simple.

Let's walk through the seven principles that shape your entire second act.

1. Improve by 1% — Not 100%

Your second act doesn't need intensity — it needs consistency.

A £20 / $20 monthly automation.

A single boundary.

One login.

Five minutes of clarity.

Small steps compound faster — and more reliably — than dramatic overhauls that crash and burn.

You're not rebuilding your financial life in one sprint.

You're rebuilding it gently, repeatedly, and sustainably.

2. Build Safety Before Strategy

Before you optimise, invest, or plan…

you stabilise.

Safety isn't optional.

It's the floor everything stands on.

A tiny emergency fund.

Basic insurance.

Clear visibility.

A calm folder of key documents.

This is the order that works in midlife:

Safety → Calm → Clarity → Strategy → Growth

This is the **Slow Money Blueprint.**

And it removes 90% of the urgency your brain tries to create.

. . .

3. One Step at a Time Is Not Slow — It's Sustainable

Your nervous system is not built for "everything at once" anymore.
One step at a time is not weakness. It's wisdom.
Order matters. Pacing matters. Your energy matters.
This isn't going slowly. This is going sustainably.

4. Move With Your Season, Not Against It

Midlife comes in seasons.
Some allow growth.
Some allow maintenance.
Some ask you to simply not fall apart.
All of them count.
Slow Money meets you exactly where you are —
not where a timeline says you "should" be.
Pressure breaks progress.
Alignment builds it.

5. Clarity Beats Hustle Every Time

You don't need more effort.
You need fewer decisions done better.
Clarity reduces panic.
Clarity reduces reactivity.
Clarity reduces self-blame.

When you know your numbers — even roughly — everything becomes less frightening.

Clarity is calm.
Calm is capacity.
Capacity is what builds wealth.

6. Calm Is a Strategy, Not a Mood

Financial calm isn't something you feel *after* everything is fixed.
It's something you cultivate while you build.
Calm is not passive.

Calm is power.
A regulated nervous system makes better long-term decisions than urgency, shame, or adrenaline ever will.
Slow Money treats calm as a financial tool — because it is.

7. You Don't Catch Up — You Return to Rhythm

Slow Money rejects the idea of "falling behind."

There is no behind.

There is only your next doable step.

Returning — again and again — to your rhythm is what creates transformation.

Not perfection.

Not intensity.

Not punishment.

Rhythm.

KEY TAKEAWAYS

- Slow wealth grows from clarity, not urgency.
- Pacing is a financial strategy.
- Safety comes before strategy — always.

Tiny Action

Choose **one**.

Not all.

Not many.

Just one — because one step is enough to shift your entire direction.

Choose the one that feels lightest on your nervous system:

□ Set up a £10/$10 weekly auto-transfer into "Security."
□ Log into **one** account — not all — simply to look.
□ Write three non-negotiables for your Second Act.
□ Put one essential bill on autopilot.

One step is a beginning.

One step is clarity.

One step is momentum.

Your second act doesn't require a transformation montage.

It requires rhythm — the kind that your life can finally hold.

You Just Built the Foundation

The Slow Money Principles you met in this chapter are not motivational slogans.

They're your grounding system.

Your reset compass.

The way you rebuild your financial life without chaos, shame, or overwhelm.

This is the moment where things begin to shift — steadily but unmistakably.

You didn't just learn a new philosophy.

You built a foundation.

A foundation that respects:

- your energy
- your season
- your responsibilities
- your limits
- your wisdom
- your future
- your truth

And now you're ready for the piece midlifers crave the most:

stability.

A grounded, solid financial floor beneath your feet.

This philosophy is the foundation for everything that follows —

the safety, systems, spending, investing, earning, and protection chapters all rest on this mindset.

And once you see money through this lens, everything becomes quieter… and clearer.

When the philosophy shifts, the systems finally make sense —

and the next chapter begins turning that philosophy into structure you can live inside.

The principles you've learned here aren't theoretical.

They become real when you apply them to your day-to-day life.

So in the next chapter, we build your Midlife Base —

the safety, breathing room, and stability your nervous system has been asking for.

This is where your financial life finally starts to feel:

- clear
- organised
- protected
- secure
- and stable enough to exhale.

PART II — REBUILD SYSTEMS

“CALM IS A FINANCIAL STRATEGY.”

CHAPTER 5
YOUR MIDLIFE BASE: YOUR FINANCIAL FLOOR OF SAFETY & STABILITY
WHY SAFETY COMES BEFORE STRATEGY

Midlife no longer gives you the luxury of chaos.
Your body doesn't tolerate it.
Your mind doesn't bounce back from it.
Your nervous system demands something different now:
stability first.
This isn't weakness.
This is wisdom.
Before you optimise anything —
before you invest, budget, plan, restructure, dream, or "get ahead" —
you build a financial floor that can hold the weight of your life.
Not a big floor.
Not a perfect floor.
A *steady* one.
Because nothing grows in instability —
not confidence, not clarity, not consistency, not wealth.

And here's the grounded reality that changes everything:

A regulated nervous system makes better financial decisions than a motivated one.

When you're overwhelmed, your brain defaults to survival mode:

- avoidance

- shame
- impulsive fixes
- catastrophising
- perfectionism
- procrastination disguised as planning

Not because you're a mess — but because you're human.

Safety interrupts that cycle.

A small buffer.

A tiny bit of breathing room.

One or two financial obligations automated.

A sense that "the basics are handled."

This quiet stability rewires your money life.

You stop bracing.

You stop dreading.

You stop spinning stories of failure.

You finally think clearly again.

When I talk about your "financial floor of safety," I mean the minimum level of stability you need to function without constant panic: a basic emergency fund, essential bills covered, protection where you'd be most exposed if life knocked sideways, and a clear view of what's coming in and going out. It's not luxury. It's the solid ground under your feet.

This chapter gives you that floor.

Not a spreadsheet.

Not a budget overhaul.

A stabilisation plan that works *with* your season, not against it.

When safety is in place, everything else becomes easier:

- investing feels doable, not scary
- pensions become clearer
- debt feels less suffocating
- boundaries come more naturally
- planning stops feeling like punishment
- money becomes less emotional, more functional

. . .

Safety is not boring.

Safety is transformation.

If you feel yourself exhaling already — that's the point.

THE FOUR PILLARS OF YOUR MIDLIFE BASE

Your Midlife Base is the floor you stand on — emotionally, financially, and practically.

It's the stability that lets you breathe again.

Not a full plan.

Not optimisation.

Not "sorting everything."

Just enough clarity and calm that your nervous system stops bracing.

These are the **four pillars** that create that floor.

They're simple on purpose — because simple is sustainable.

PILLAR 1 — Visibility (Seeing What's True)

You can't lead your financial life if you can't *see* your financial life.

Visibility isn't spreadsheets, colour coding, or perfection.

It's simply:

- You know what you have.
- You know what you owe.
- You know what comes in.
- You know what goes out.
- You know where things actually live.

Visibility removes fear because fear thrives in the unknown.

Visibility isn't a task — it's a relationship.

A five-minute "look, don't judge" ritual each week builds more financial safety than three hours of panicked sorting.

Visibility creates orientation.

Orientation creates calm.

Calm creates better decisions.

PILLAR 2 — Safety (Stability Before Strategy)

Midlife doesn't reward risk-taking.

Midlife rewards stability.

Safety is the foundation the rest of your financial life stands on.

Safety looks like:

- A small emergency buffer *(£300–£1,000 / $300–$1,000 — enough to breathe)*
- Your essential bills categorised
- Your income streams accounted for
- Basic protection in place (UK: emergency fund + pension + insurance; US: emergency fund + 401(k)/IRA + insurance)
- A clear sense of **what it costs to be you each month** *(rough is enough)*

Safety = breathing room.

Safety says:

"I can handle a shock without falling apart."

This is the calm that makes everything else possible.

PILLAR 3 — Systems (Your Life on Autopilot)

Midlife is too busy, too demanding, too emotionally full for you to manage money manually.

Systems do the heavy lifting so you don't have to.

Systems look like:

- Bills automated
- Minimum payments automated
- A savings or investment direct debit (even £20/$20)
- A weekly 10-minute check-in
- Digital folders or notes for key documents
- One home for your passwords/logins

Systems turn chaos into rhythm.

When systems hold you, you stop white-knuckling your financial life.

You don't rely on motivation.

You rely on structure.

Systems protect tired days, busy weeks, and emotional seasons.

PILLAR 4 — Breathing Room (Creating Space, Not Pressure)

This is the pillar nearly every midlifer forgets.

Breathing room is the emotional and financial space where sustainable decisions live.

Breathing room looks like:

- One small gap in your calendar
- One small gap in your budget
- One place where you stop over-functioning
- One thing removed from your plate
- One expectation lowered
- One responsibility shared or delegated
- One subscription cancelled
- One boundary reclaimed

Breathing room softens your nervous system enough to take action.

Without breathing room, everything feels urgent.

Urgency triggers freeze.

Freeze kills momentum.

Breathing room is not laziness.

It's capacity-building.

It's where Slow Money truly begins.

"With a steady base beneath me, even the smallest step feels safe."

Why These Four Pillars Matter

Most financial books start at the top of the pyramid — budgeting, investing, optimisation.

This book starts at the bottom.

Because without:

- visibility
- safety
- systems
- breathing room

…you will keep cycling through overwhelm → shame → avoidance → panic.

These four pillars stop that cycle.

They stabilise you.

They support you.

They steady the ground beneath you.

And once you're steady, everything else becomes doable — calmly, consistently, sustainably.

Now that the foundation is clear, here's the truth:

Most midlifers *know* these four pillars matter —

so why haven't they been able to build them?

Not laziness.

Not irresponsibility.

Not lack of discipline.

Not poor character.

The answer is rooted in:

- survival mode
- overwhelm
- responsibility overload
- emotional fatigue
- outdated systems
- frozen nervous systems
- shame cycles
- unclear next steps

And that's exactly what we address next.

THE OBSTACLE LAYER (WHY THIS HASN'T WORKED BEFORE)

Most midlifers don't struggle with money because they're careless.

They struggle because the systems they were taught were never built for real life.

Before we build your Midlife Base, we need to name the obstacles that stopped you before —

not to shame you, but to free you.

Once you understand why old strategies failed, you stop blaming yourself…

and you finally stop repeating patterns that were never yours to fix.

Let's lay the truth out clearly.

1. You were taught intensity, not consistency.

Everything in traditional financial advice screams:

"Do more."

"Cut more."

"Save more."

"Work harder."

"Sacrifice now."

But intensity collapses the moment life becomes real:

A sick parent.

A child needing support.

A job restructure.

A bad month.

A burnout flare.

A surprise bill.

Chaos breaks intensity every time.

Slow Money thrives because it doesn't ask for intensity.

It asks for repeatable, humane consistency — the only thing a midlife nervous system can hold.

2. You tried to build wealth on top of exhaustion.

You weren't unmotivated.

You were depleted.

Depletion makes even simple financial tasks feel enormous.

When your body is in survival mode, your brain prioritises:

- getting through the day
- avoiding more stress
- staying functional

Not opening pension dashboards.

Not reviewing subscriptions.

Not reorganising budgets.

You weren't avoiding money.

You were avoiding *overwhelm*.

And overwhelm always wins…

until you build safety first.

3. You were managing other people's needs above your own.

Midlife is a convergence of responsibilities:

- Kids
- Teens
- Adult children
- Ageing parents
- Partners
- Work
- Home
- Life admin
- Invisible labour

Some months you're running two households.

Some months you're the emotional centre of everyone else's crisis.

Financial clarity cannot thrive in a life where your energy is constantly being drafted into other people's emergencies.

You didn't fail.

You were over-stretched.

. . .

4. Your financial systems were built for your younger self — not your current life.

A younger you signed up for:

- subscriptions you stopped using
- budgets you outgrew
- jobs you've outlived
- habits that no longer fit
- timelines created before you understood your real needs

Your life evolved.

Your systems didn't.

Mismatch creates chaos.

Slow Money is the first system designed specifically for your *midlife self* —

the wiser, stretched, discerning version of you that needs clarity, not clutter.

5. You expected motivation to get you through — and motivation always disappears.

It spikes.

It crashes.

It evaporates.

You didn't stay "disciplined" because motivation isn't designed to be sustainable.

Systems are.

Tiny, repeatable behaviours are.

Calm routines are.

Motivation is a spark.

Systems are the stove.

6. You thought you needed confidence first.

You waited for confidence before acting.

Midlife finally shows the truth:

Confidence is the *result* of taking small steps —

not the prerequisite.

You weren't stuck because you lacked discipline.

You were stuck because you believed you had to feel ready.

Slow Money removes that barrier.

7. Shame kept you in the dark.

Avoidance isn't laziness — it's protection.

Every time you felt behind, embarrassed, or confused, the shame made the task heavier.

So you avoided looking.

Not because you're irresponsible…

but because you're human.

Shame blocks clarity.

Clarity dissolves shame.

This chapter is about dissolving it — permanently.

8. You tried to jump to "advanced" strategies without building a base.

You were told you "should" be investing.

So you froze because you didn't feel ready.

You were told you "should" have a 6-month emergency fund.

So you froze because you had none.

You were told you "should" understand pensions.

So you froze because you didn't.

You weren't failing.

You were starting from a foundation you were never taught to build.

Slow Money fixes this by building **your Midlife Base first** —
the safety floor your nervous system and future rely on.

What This Means

You didn't fail at money.
You were using systems that were:

- too intense
- too fast
- too unrealistic

- too demanding
- too shame-driven
- too disconnected from real life

Your second act starts with something entirely different:

A base that fits *you*.

A pace that honours *you*.

A philosophy that respects *you*.

Now that we've cleared the obstacles,

we can finally build the structure everything rests on.

A Midlife Base in Real Life: Carla, 49

Carla, 49, had three credit cards, a variable income, and a constant hum of money anxiety. For years she told herself she'd "sort it out properly" when life calmed down – it never did.

When she finally built her Midlife Base, she did three small things:

- listed every account and debt on a single page
- set up autopay for her mortgage, council tax, and minimum card payments
- started a £40 monthly transfer into a "Security" pot

Nothing dramatic happened overnight – but the 3am panic began to ease. For the first time, she knew exactly what went out each month, and that the essentials would be paid even on tired days. Six months later, that tiny security pot had become a real buffer, and the "I'm a mess with money" story had started to loosen its grip.

Next: The Midlife Base Plan — Your Foundation for Calm Wealth

This is where your financial life becomes:

- clear
- stable
- organized
- doable
- and emotionally safe

This is where the overwhelm ends and steadiness begins.

YOUR MIDLIFE BASE PLAN (STEP-BY-STEP FRAMEWORK)

The Calm, Steady Foundation Your Second Act Needs

Before you optimise, invest, or get ambitious —

you stabilise.

This is where your financial system becomes something your nervous system can actually hold. No more chaotic juggling, no more "hope it sorts itself out," no more 2am panic spirals.

This is your **Midlife Base Plan** — the step-by-step framework that gives you steadiness, clarity, and breathing room.

Not hustle.

Not pressure.

Just a structure that supports you.

A four-step, calm-first method for stabilising your financial life

This is the floor everything else stands on.

It's intentionally simple — because simplicity is what your life can hold right now.

STEP 1 — Ground Yourself (Your Reality Check Ritual)

Before you move anything, you **look**.

This is not a budgeting task.

It's a stabilising one.

Do this once — gently:

1 List all accounts (pensions, savings, credit cards, loans)

2 Write approximate balances (rounding is fine)

3 Circle anything that feels "unclear," "messy," or "unknown"

4 Put a star next to anything that feels surprisingly okay

This process is about **orientation**, not judgement.

You can't build a second act from avoidance — only from awareness.

. . .

Slow Money Truth:

Clarity is emotional regulation.

STEP 2 — Build Your Safety Layer (Your Non-Negotiable Essentials)

This layer protects you from shocks — the things that knock midlifers sideways.

Your safety layer includes:

✔ **A Starter Emergency Fund**

£300–£1,000 / $300–$1,000

(Just enough to prevent panic and debt spirals.)

✔ **Essential Insurance Check** (appropriate to your country and circumstances)

- Life cover (if someone depends on you)
- Income protection or disability cover
- Health insurance (US)
- Basic home/renters insurance

✔ **Auto-pay for the Absolute Musts**

Set auto-pay for:

- rent/mortgage
- utilities
- council tax / property tax
- minimum debt payments

This isn't indulgence.

This is **capacity creation**.

Safety → Calm → Clarity → Strategy.

STEP 3 — Create Your Calm Systems (The Rhythm That Keeps You Steady)

This is where life gets easier.

You design systems that run even when you're tired, overwhelmed, or emotionally done.

✔ **One Weekly Money Ritual (10 minutes)**

Same time, same day.

A gentle check-in, not a problem-solving session.

✔ **One Automation for Savings**

£10–£50 weekly

or

£40–£200 monthly

(Choose a number your nervous system won't flinch at.)

✔ **A Single Spending Structure**

Not a budget.

A rhythm:

- Bills
- Essentials
- Flex
- Future You (savings/investing)

Simple. Sustainable. Repeatable.

STEP 4 — Stabilise Your Cashflow (The Midlife-Friendly Method)

Stability comes from predictability.

You're not trying to "cut everything."

You're trying to **make everything smoother**.

You do this by:

✔ **Identifying Your "Steady Costs"**

The things that don't change monthly:

- housing
- transport
- food
- childcare
- insurance
- essential subscriptions

✔ **Smoothing Your Fluctuating Costs**

Annual bills → divided into 12 and automated

Seasonal expenses → added into a "sinking fund"

Birthdays/Christmas → planned, not panicked

✔ **Naming Your Money Drains**

Not to shame — to choose consciously.

Midlife is all about deliberate spending.

. . .

STEP 5 — Prepare for the Next Layer (Your Ready Point)

This step tells you you're ready to move deeper into the journey.

You are ready for the next chapter when these are true:

✔ You know roughly what you have
✔ Your essential bills are stable
✔ You have a tiny emergency buffer
✔ You are no longer avoiding accounts
✔ You feel emotionally safer around money
✔ You feel even a *little* more agency
✔ Your week has a money ritual rhythm
✔ You have one saving or investing automation set
✔ You don't feel panicked every time you think about money

This is enough. More than enough to move forward.

This is the point where readers stop spiralling
and start breathing.

This is the floor on which we build everything else.

KEY TAKEAWAYS

• A strong financial base begins with stability and breathing room.

• Safety nets and essentials come before optimisation, investing, or "getting ahead."

• Even a small, steady floor of security can soften money anxiety and help you exhale.

Tiny Action

Choose one:

□ Put one essential bill on autopilot.
□ Set up a £10/$10 weekly transfer.
□ Start a sinking fund for one annual expense.

□ Pick your weekly money ritual day & time.
□ Write down your "steady costs".

One step is momentum.
Momentum is transformation.

Once your base starts to feel steadier, the next step is changing how money moves through your day-to-day life — calmly. That's where the Calm Money Method comes in.

Next, in Chapter 6, we bring you something powerful:

Your Nervous-System-Friendly Budget: Spending Peace & Enoughness

A budgeting method that doesn't punish you —
it supports you.

"PEACE IS A FORM OF PROFIT."

CHAPTER 6
THE CALM MONEY METHOD™
WHAT CALM MONEY ACTUALLY IS.

A *Nervous-System-Friendly Way to Handle Money in Midlife*

Calm Money isn't about feeling relaxed while you deal with money.

It's about creating the conditions where clarity becomes possible.

It's the opposite of panic money — the kind that makes you:

- avoid your accounts
- make rushed decisions
- overspend to cope
- under-save because you "can't deal"
- freeze until things get worse

Calm Money is a **nervous-system-aware approach** to your financial life.

Not soft.

Not passive.

Not "good vibes only."

It's practical, structured, and designed for midlife — the season where your body, brain, and bandwidth demand a different way of doing things.

Calm Money means:

- You reduce financial noise so your brain can think.
- You create predictability where life allows it.
- You act from steadiness, not threat mode.

- You move slowly enough to see what's actually happening.
- You build structure that supports your energy, not drains it.

Calm isn't a personality trait.

Calm is a financial strategy.

Because clarity only shows up when your system feels safe enough to look.

Calm Money asks one question:

"What do I need now so I can think clearly?"

Not forever.

Not for the whole plan.

Just for the next step.

Asked consistently, that single question changes everything.

Micro-Action

Take 30 seconds and ask yourself:

"What would make money feel 5% calmer this week?"

Not fixed.

Not sorted.

Just calmer.

Pick one thought:

- "I don't have to rush."
- "I'm allowed to learn slowly."
- "Clarity comes from gentleness."
- "I don't need to solve everything today."

This is how we begin.

Why Calm Money Beats Panic Money

Panic money feels urgent.

Calm money feels intelligent.

When you're overwhelmed, the instinct is always the same:

Fix it fast.

Do everything at once.

Make a dramatic plan.

Burn through adrenaline and hope it sticks.

Adrenaline-based money decisions have two outcomes:

1 Burnout

2 Regret

Panic creates loops:

- emotional spending
- avoidance
- over-optimisation
- frantic spreadsheets
- all-or-nothing plans
- "I'll start again Monday"
- financial self-blame

Calm breaks those loops — and replaces them with rhythm.

Why Calm Works Better

1. Calm creates clarity.

Panic narrows your thinking. Calm widens it.

2. Calm builds consistency.

Intensity burns out. Consistency compounds.

3. Calm preserves energy.

Panic drains capacity. Calm keeps you in motion.

4. Calm reduces mistakes.

Panic overcommits. Calm chooses deliberately.

5. Calm supports your system.

This isn't mindset — it's biology.

A regulated system makes better decisions.

6. Calm turns money into leadership.

Panic says: *"I've messed this up."*

Calm says: *"I'm leading myself."*

Leadership always wins.

The Quiet Midlife Advantage

Youth relies on energy.

Midlife relies on insight.

Calm lets you use what you've earned:

- pattern recognition
- boundaries
- lived wisdom
- self-knowledge

Calm isn't passive.

Calm isn't naïve.

Calm is grounded power.

And now, with the *why* in place, we move into the engine of this chapter.

The Calm Money Method™

Awareness → Clarity → Choice → Action → Return

Calm Money isn't a feeling.

It's a **repeatable rhythm** — one you return to whenever life shifts, numbers wobble, or emotions spike.

This is the Calm Money Method™.

Simple by design — because your system can hold simple.

STEP 1 — Awareness

"What's true right now?"

This is your pause point.

Not fixing.

Not planning.

Just noticing.

Awareness sounds like:

- "I feel anxious about money."
- "I'm avoiding that account."
- "Something feels off."

Awareness is never judgement.

It's orientation.

Tiny step:

Open one account. Just look.

STEP 2 — Clarity

"What actually matters right now?"

Clarity turns emotional fog into something you can hold.

Clarity looks like:

- listing accounts
- noting essentials
- checking balances (rough is fine)
- naming top stressors

Panic lives in vagueness.
Clarity shrinks the threat.

Tiny step:

Choose one clarity task. One is enough.

STEP 3 — Choice

"What's the next right thing?"

Choice dissolves overwhelm.
You don't fix everything — you choose one thing that matters most.
Examples:

- "This month I build a mini emergency fund."
- "This week I automate £20/$20."
- "Today I cancel two subscriptions."

Choice gives your tired brain direction.

If debt is your biggest stressor, this is where **Snowball Plus**™ comes in — our calm, human method for paying it down without panic or punishment.

Tiny step:

Ask: *"What would help the most with the least stress?"*

STEP 4 — Action

Low-pressure movement

Action is not intensity.
It's one small, doable move:

- one automation
- one transfer
- one login
- one boundary
- one payment

Tiny steps build consistency.
Consistency builds capacity.
Capacity builds confidence.

Tiny step:

Take one 2-minute action before your brain talks you out of it.

• • •

STEP 5 — Return

Come back — don't catch up

This is the heart of Calm Money.
You don't need perfection.
You don't need momentum.
You don't need to stay "on track."
You just return.
Awareness → Clarity → Choice → Action → Return.
Again.
And again.
And again.
Return builds rhythm.
Rhythm builds calm.
Calm builds wealth.

If Debt Is the Fire: Snowball Plus™ (Quick Start)

Snowball Plus™ is the Slow Money™ way to stabilise debt.
You list debts from smallest to largest.
You keep paying minimums on all.
Any extra goes to one target balance.
Why it works:

- progress feels achievable
- motivation stays alive
- shame drops
- follow-through improves

It's not mathematically perfect —
it's **humanly sustainable**.
And sustainability wins in midlife.

What's Next

You've calmed the noise.

Now we explore **spending peace** — not restriction, not shame, but truth.

Because spending peace doesn't begin with numbers.

It begins with understanding what your body is carrying.

Tiny Step

Set a weekly 10-minute Calm Money Ritual.
This is your anchor.

KEY TAKEAWAYS

- The Calm Money Method™ gives you a repeatable, nervous-system–safe rhythm for handling money.
- Awareness → Clarity → Choice → Action → Return is your new default loop when things feel overwhelming.
- Snowball Plus helps you stabilise debt at a human pace, prioritising follow-through and calm momentum over mathematical perfection.

THE PAYOFF MOMENT — What This Method Gives You

When you use the Calm Money Method, you gain:

- a calmer nervous system
- a structured pathway out of financial freeze
- confidence built from real consistency
- a clear understanding of your priorities
- a sense of agency you haven't felt in years
- sustainable progress without burnout
- a money system that grows with you, not against you

This is the moment where you stop spiralling and start steering.
This is where Quiet Wealth begins.

You've calmed your financial overwhelm from the inside out — now we move into spending. Not numbers first, but truth first. Because spending peace doesn't begin with restriction. It begins with understanding what your body is carrying.

• • •

You've learned how to calm the noise — now we shift into understanding the deeper patterns underneath your spending.

In the next chapter, we'll explore the roots of "enoughness," the emotional hunger behind over-spending, and the steady habits that build real spending peace — not restriction, not shame, just truth.

"I DON'T NEED TO RUSH — I NEED TO CONTINUE."

CHAPTER 7
SPENDING PEACE & ENOUGHNESS
WHY MIDLIFE SPENDING ISN'T "LACK OF DISCIPLINE" (THE REAL STORY)

A Nervous-System-Friendly Spending Method for Midlife

There's a type of spending almost nobody talks about — not the dramatic shopping-spree kind, but the quiet kind.

The kind that happens when you're tired to the bone.

The kind that whispers:

"I've held everything together today — I deserve one small thing."

"I need something to feel good for a minute."

"I can't carry one more decision."

"I just want softness… somewhere."

This isn't greed. It isn't impulsiveness. And it's definitely not irresponsibility.

It's **fatigue spending** — the emotional bill your system sends when it's been holding too much for too long, without enough support.

And in midlife, that makes perfect sense.

Because midlife isn't just "life." It's layered life: responsibilities, caregiving, shifting identity, rising costs — and the quiet pressure of feeling like you should have it all figured out by now.

So if spending has become emotional, it's not because you're broken.

It's because you're carrying more than most systems were designed for.

Here's the truth midlifers need to hear on repeat:

Most overspending isn't recklessness. It's depletion.

And once you stop treating depletion like a character flaw, everything becomes easier to change.

This chapter is not about restriction.

It's about **Spending Peace™** — spending with dignity, self-respect, and alignment.

A pace of money your midlife capacity can actually hold.

Why Midlife Spending Gets So Emotional

Spending becomes emotional when life requires emotional endurance.

When your day is full of invisible labour — holding everyone together, keeping the household moving, staying functional through stress — your brain looks for relief.

Not joy. Relief.

Midlife emotional spending usually comes from one of these needs:

- **Rest** (you're running on empty)
- **Relief** (your stress needs an exit)
- **Comfort** (you need softness somewhere)
- **Connection** (loneliness feels loud)
- **Control** (life feels unpredictable)
- **Numbness** (you can't process one more thing)

This isn't immaturity.

It's emotional first aid.

And there's also a biological layer: when you're stressed, your system shifts into fight / flight / freeze / fawn — and each state has a money behaviour attached.

- **Fight:** "I deserve this."
- **Flight:** "I need to fix this fast."
- **Freeze:** "I can't look. I can't deal."
- **Fawn:** "I'll just say yes — it's easier."

So the goal isn't to shame the behaviour.

The goal is to **change the state** underneath it.

Because spending habits don't reveal your worth.

They reveal your **capacity**.

The One Rule That Changes Everything

Regulate first. Decide second.

If you make spending decisions in fatigue, stress, or overwhelm, you'll default to soothing instead of choosing.

So we're going to give you two tools:

1 a **10-second** "in-the-moment" reset, and

2 a **10-minute weekly ritual** that turns Spending Peace into a habit.

The In-The-Moment Tool

PAUSE → NAME → CHOOSE

Use this any time you feel the urge to buy from stress, tiredness, or emotional noise.

1) PAUSE (10 seconds)

Hand on chest. Slow exhale. Shoulders down.

One sentence:

"I choose from alignment, not adrenaline."

You don't need a meditation. You just need a tiny nervous-system shift.

2) NAME (the real need)

Ask:

"What feeling am I trying to buy?"

Common answers: rest, comfort, connection, control, relief.

Naming the need loosens the urge, because the brain stops treating the purchase as "the only option."

3) CHOOSE (one aligned action)

Now choose one of these:

- If it's **rest** → take five minutes off your feet
- If it's **comfort** → warmth, tea, blanket, shower
- If it's **connection** → one message or voice note
- If it's **control** → write one small next step
- If it's **relief** → breathe + delay purchase by 24 hours

You're not "being strict."

You're being intelligent.

This is Spending Peace in real time.

The Midlife Spending Map™

Your 10-Minute Weekly Ritual for Spending Peace

Budgets fail when they demand control.

This works because it builds **capacity** instead.

This isn't a spreadsheet marathon. It's a grounded practice — a rhythm you can return to even during busy weeks and tired seasons.

Set a timer for ten minutes.

1) Ground (1 minute)

Hand on chest. One breath. One sentence:

"I'm here to understand, not judge."

2) Glance (2 minutes)

Open your banking app. Scroll last week's spending.

That's it.

You are training your system:

"Money is safe to look at."

3) Celebrate (2 minutes)

Mark three purchases that felt aligned — even small ones.

Aligned means: it supported your wellbeing, values, responsibilities, or future.

This rewires the identity story from:

"I'm bad with money" → "I already make good choices."

4) Reflect (2 minutes)

Choose **one** purchase that felt misaligned (only one).

Ask:

Was I tired? overwhelmed? lonely? stressed? trying to buy relief?

No shame. Just pattern recognition.

5) Refine (2 minutes)

Make **one** micro-tweak for next week.

Examples:

- add one rest ritual so you don't spend to soothe
- delete one shopping app
- cancel one subscription
- set a "24-hour pause" rule for late-night purchases
- add *intentional joy* (to prevent burnout spending)

6) Anchor (1 minute)

Close with identity:

"I spend in alignment with who I am becoming."

That's the Map.

Ten minutes. One tweak. Repeat.

This is how spending changes without self-attack.

• • •

Enoughness

The Quiet Superpower Behind Spending Peace

Enoughness isn't deprivation.

It isn't minimalism.

It isn't becoming a smaller version of yourself.

In midlife, **Enoughness is sovereignty**.

It's the moment you stop measuring life by "more" and start measuring it by alignment.

Enoughness says:

"I no longer spend from exhaustion, performance, or comparison. I spend from who I am now."

The Enoughness Questions (Weekly, not per purchase)

Ask once a week:

- What gives me peace?
- What quietly drains me?
- What feels like self-respect?
- What am I buying because I'm tired?
- What am I buying because it truly matters?

These questions don't micromanage you.

They *anchor* you.

Enoughness doesn't remove joy.

It makes joy intentional — and removes the "soothing spend" cycle that creates regret.

KEY TAKEAWAYS

- Calm spending isn't about restriction — it's about regulation and relief.
- Enoughness shifts you from impulse → alignment, and from pressure → presence.
- Your spending becomes grounded when it reflects identity, not emotion.
- Replacement, not removal, keeps your nervous system safe and reduces rebellion.
- Enoughness is midlife power: the moment spending stops being a coping strategy.

. . .

Tiny Action

Choose ONE (nervous-system safe)

- □ Do **PAUSE → NAME → CHOOSE** once this week before a purchase
- □ Schedule your **10-minute Spending Map** (day + time)
- □ Pick one "Enoughness edge" for the week: one gentle boundary, one intentional joy

Reflection Prompt — You've Done Hard Things

You've faced storms before. This one doesn't define you. Breathe. Begin from strength.

You're no longer buying to soothe exhaustion.

You're spending from alignment, clarity, and self-respect.

You are leading your spending — gently, consistently, intentionally.

This is not smaller living.

This is sovereign living.

And as you practice the Spending Map, your financial life begins to feel like something you can *trust* — because it starts to reflect the person you're becoming.

Spending Peace isn't a goal.

It's a practice.

A rhythm.

A reclamation.

And you have already begun.

Next Chapter: Investing as Midlife Security & Self-Respect

. . .

Now that your spending is grounded and clear, you are ready for the gentlest, most empowering investing chapter you've ever read.

We go slow.

We go steady.

We build safety, not stress.

PAUSE HERE.

Drop your shoulders.

Nothing in this chapter is urgent.

Come back into your body before we continue.

"MY TIMELINE IS SACRED."

CHAPTER 8

INVESTING AS MIDLIFE SECURITY & SELF-RESPECT

THE EMOTIONAL DOORWAY INTO INVESTING.

Evan was 52 the first time he opened his investing account and simply… stared.

Not trading.

Not analysing.

Not doing anything "wrong."

Just sitting with the weight of a lifetime of: *I should have figured this out by now.*

For years, he assumed investing belonged to other people — the earlier, the sharper, the naturally confident. People who learned pensions at the kitchen table. People who didn't feel their stomach drop at the word *markets.*

He also believed there was an age where the door shuts. Where someone would tap him on the shoulder and say:

Sorry. You're too late.

So when he finally opened his pension dashboard — hands slightly shaking — he didn't feel proud.

He felt grief.

Grief for the years he wishes he'd understood more.

Grief for the choices made while juggling real life, not reading finance books.

Grief for the younger version of himself who wasn't clueless — just overwhelmed, unsupported, and trying to hold everything together.

Then something shifted. Not a dramatic breakthrough — a quiet settling.

Okay. I'm here now.

And that was the real beginning.

Not the first contribution.

Not the growth chart.

Not the buzzword clarity.

The beginning was the moment he stopped treating his future like a threat.

That's where this chapter meets you.

Before we go further: this chapter is here to help you understand how investing works — not to tell you what to buy. All investments rise and fall, and nothing here is a recommendation for any specific fund, platform, or product. Think of this as calm clarity: a grounded starting point for decisions that fit your own life.

The Midlife Myth: "I've Left It Too Late"

Midlife has a way of making the clock feel louder.

Not because you've actually run out of time — but because for the first time, time feels real.

The fear isn't mathematical. It's emotional. It's mourning the years you were too stretched, too tired, too deep in survival mode to think about investing. It's wishing your younger self had felt safer, more informed, more supported.

But here's the truth:

You didn't fail your younger self.

Your younger self carried you here.

They were navigating work, caretaking, bills, health surprises, breakups, burnout — a world that taught survival, not investing. They weren't irresponsible. They were overloaded.

And now?

Now you're ready in a way you simply weren't then.

Midlife investing isn't about catching up. It's about catching your breath. It's shifting from fear-based avoidance to grounded participation — replacing:

"I'm late"

with
"I'm here now — and that matters."
"Late" is a shame story, not a financial reality.
Nothing about investing closes at 40.
Nothing closes at 50.
Nothing closes at 60 and beyond.
The only thing that closes is the chapter where fear makes decisions for you.
And clarity compounds faster than youth.

What Investing Actually Is (Without the Noise)

You've been taught your whole life that investing is complicated.
Charts.
Jargon.
People shouting on TV.
Friends bragging about "winning big."
Headlines predicting disaster every ten minutes.
All of it creates the same internal story: *This world is for people who know more than I do.*
But the quiet truth is simpler:
Investing is owning tiny pieces of real businesses and letting time grow them.
That's it.
Not gambling.
Not guessing winners.
Not timing the market.
Not day-trading with three screens and a heart rate monitor.
When you invest, you're participating in human progress — businesses solving problems, selling products, earning profits. Your little slice grows alongside it.
Most people don't struggle with investing because they lack intelligence. They struggle because of:

- fear
- headlines
- volatility
- the feeling of "not knowing enough"

• shame around starting late

This chapter rewrites that.

You will not be rushed.

You will not be spoken down to.

You will not be shamed.

You will not be overwhelmed.

You will learn to invest through clarity, repetition, and tiny steps — until investing stops feeling like a threat and starts feeling like what it is:

Self-protection.

A quiet way of saying: *My future deserves stability, dignity, and choice.*

The Two Things That Actually Matter

Strip away the hype and there are only two forces that shape long-term outcomes:

1) Time in the Market

Your money grows because it stays invested — not because you constantly adjust, chase, or tweak.

Compounding is simple:

- your money earns money
- then that money earns money
- then growth earns growth
- and over time, the curve bends upward

Compounding doesn't only reward early starts.

It rewards steadiness.

And midlife gives you steadiness in spades.

2) Staying Invested

Markets drop.

Markets rise.

They drop again.

They rise higher over time.

This isn't unusual. It's the nature of long-term growth.

What hurts returns isn't the drop — it's the panic exit.

Most people lose decades of growth because a headline scared them.

But midlifers are built differently now. You've lived through crises. You've rebuilt after setbacks. You understand emotional waves.

Your superpower isn't speed.

It's emotional maturity.

And emotional maturity is one of the strongest investing skills there is.

THE SLOW MONEY INVESTING FRAMEWORK™

Midlife investing needs a third path: calm, simple, sustainable wealth-building that works with real life — not adrenaline.

This framework is built on six truths:

- your energy matters as much as your numbers
- safety creates better decisions than urgency
- simplicity beats complexity every time
- consistency — not cleverness — compounds your future
- calm is an advantage most late starters underestimate
- a steady plan is more powerful than a perfect plan

Here's the framework:

1) Keep it simple — and deliberately boring

Boring investing outperforms emotional investing.

One or two globally diversified funds can build an entire future.

2) Automate everything you can

Motivation comes and goes. Systems don't.

Automation protects you from mood, fear, headlines, procrastination, and perfectionism.

3) Build stability before strategy

You invest best when you feel steady, not stretched.

Before you invest meaningfully, stabilise:

- a small emergency buffer
- minimum debt payments
- predictable bills
- a short weekly money ritual
- breathing room

4) Ignore the noise (seriously)

Your timeframe is decades, not days.

Mantra: If my heart rate rises, I close the news — not my account.

5) Review annually — not emotionally

Constant checking creates cortisol. Annual review creates clarity.

6) Stay invested — through everything

Drops aren't danger. They're normal movement.

Your advantage is staying steady.

This framework protects your bandwidth, your mental health, and your future self — turning investing from a threat into a rhythm.

Understanding Risk (Without Panic)

Risk isn't danger.

Risk is movement.

Markets breathe. They pulse. They move like a tide — not like a threat.

Risk becomes harmful when it triggers emotional exits.

So here's the Slow Money reframe:

You don't remove risk. You right-size risk to your life.

Ask yourself:

- How would I feel if my investments fell 10–20% this year?
- Would I be able to leave the money alone?
- What pace feels kind to my body?
- What amount feels safe to invest right now?

If your body tightens, you lower the amount or choose a steadier mix.

If your body exhales, you increase slowly.

There is no moral success in taking on more risk than your nervous system can hold.

Calm investors tend to outperform panicked investors — not because they're smarter, but because they stay invested.

Asset Allocation (Explained Like a Human)

Asset allocation is simply:

The mix that makes you feel safe enough to stay invested.

- Shares (equities) = growth (more movement)
- Bonds = stability (smoother ride)

The "right" allocation isn't what someone online calls optimal.

It's what you can live with during a wobble.

A calm starting point for many midlifers:

- 60–80% shares
- 20–40% bonds

If that feels too spicy, start 50/50.

There is zero shame in steadiness.

Consistency beats bravery every time.

Choosing the Right Account (UK & US)

You only need one good home to begin. Not five.

Choose the account that gives you the most tax benefit, the most ease, and the most long-term calm.

If you're in the UK

1) Pension (Workplace Pension or SIPP)

Priority because:

- tax relief (free money)
- employer matching (often more free money)
- tax-advantaged growth
- long-term structure

Best for: long-term security and retirement income.

2) Stocks & Shares ISA

The most flexible, stress-free investing account for many midlifers:

- tax-free growth
- tax-free withdrawals
- no penalties for access
- excellent for your Future Me Fund and midlife goals

A pension + S&S ISA is the UK dream team.

If you're in the US

1) 401(k) (or 403(b) / TSP)

If your employer matches contributions, that match is free money. Take it.

Benefits include:

- potential match
- tax advantages (traditional or Roth options depending on plan)
- automated consistency through payroll

2) IRA (Roth or Traditional)

Choose based on your tax bracket and plans:

- Roth IRA: tax now, withdrawals later are tax-free (subject to rules)
- Traditional IRA: potential tax relief now, tax later on withdrawals

Only after these are funded do you consider a taxable brokerage account — and only if you need one.

One strong container → one consistent habit → one future you can trust.

Choosing Your Fund (One Fund Can Build Your Future)

A good fund should be:

- global
- diversified
- low-cost
- long-term friendly
- simple to automate
- emotionally safe

Your Slow Money rule:

One fund can build my whole future.

UK examples (widely used, not prescriptions)

- Vanguard FTSE Global All Cap
- Vanguard LifeStrategy (e.g., 60 or 80, depending on risk comfort)
- HSBC FTSE All-World
- BlackRock Global Index

Ethical / ESG examples:

- Legal & General Future World range
- FTSE All-World ESG funds
- Vanguard ESG Global All Cap (or similar ESG global index options)

US examples (widely used, not prescriptions)

- Vanguard Total World (VT)
- Vanguard Total Stock Market (VTI)
- S&P 500 funds (VOO or equivalents)
- Schwab / Fidelity equivalents

Ethical / ESG examples:

- iShares ESG Aware funds (various)
- Fidelity sustainability index options
- Schwab sustainable equity options
- Vanguard socially responsible / ESG equivalents (where available)

Note: fund names, tickers, and availability can change. Always check the most up-to-date information on your platform before investing.

The Late-Starter Path (Age 40–60+)

You are not "late."

You are seasoned.

And readiness outperforms youth every single time.

Here's the calm path:

1) Stabilise before you invest

- small emergency buffer (even £100/$100 starts the signal)
- minimum debt payments covered
- bills predictable
- a short weekly money ritual
- breathing room

2) Automate tiny contributions

Start tiny on purpose:

- £10 / £20 / £25
- $10 / $25

The amount matters less than the identity shift:

I am someone who invests now.

3) Use one simple fund

Global index fund, balanced fund, target-date fund, or ESG equivalent.

One calm home. No complexity jungle.

4) Increase slowly and kindly

Not from guilt. Not from pressure.

Increase in whispers:

- +£5 / +£10
- +1% pension contribution
- a small bump when a bill disappears

5) Ignore headlines

You are building decades, not reacting to drama.

6) Review once a year

Tea. Calm. One look. One gentle adjustment.

7) Anchor everything in self-respect

You're not investing to impress anyone.

You're investing for dignity.

Your Weekly Investor Ritual (Five Minutes)

Confidence comes from familiarity — not from knowing everything.

Once a week. Five minutes. No drama.

Step 1 — Arrive (30 seconds)

Breathe. Drop your shoulders. Say softly:

My money is safe with me.

Step 2 — Log in (1 minute)

Open your pension / ISA / 401(k) / IRA. Just look.

You're training your system: Money is safe to look at.

Step 3 — One tiny action (2 minutes)

Choose one:

- add £5–£10 / $5–$10
- check your contribution percentage
- confirm your fund choice is still correct
- read one line of your statement
- rename your account something grounding (Future Me Fund / Calm Wealth Pot)

Step 4 — Anchor (30 seconds)

I invest with calm consistency.

Step 5 — Close (1 minute)

Log out. Close tabs. Walk away.

No doom-scrolling. No research spiral.

You showed up. That is enough.

Choose ONE Tiny Step Today

Only one. Because we're building identity, not intensity.

- Open your investing/pension dashboard and look for 20 seconds
- Set (or check) an automatic monthly contribution
- Increase an existing contribution by £5/$5 or 1%
- Write your chosen fund name somewhere safe
- Schedule your annual review date
- Delete one unused shopping app
- Say aloud: I am allowed to learn this at my age

One tiny step — repeated — becomes a lifetime of calm wealth.

Risk-Calming Scripts

When markets wobble:

- Markets fall. Markets rise. I stay steady.
- This feeling is temporary. My plan is long-term.
- Volatility isn't danger — it's movement.
- Dips are normal. My strategy is calm.

When you want to sell in panic:

- I don't make long-term decisions in short-term emotions.
- Fear is a feeling, not a financial instruction.
- This is noise, not a signal.
- My future self will thank me for staying invested.

Pick one sentence that lands in your chest, not just your head:

Steady is safe.

Calm investors win.

Slow money grows.

Ethical & Values-Based Investing (Optional)

Ethical investing isn't moral perfection.

It's simple alignment:

I want my money to grow in a way that feels right for who I am.

The calmest approach:

Choose the ethical version of the fund you already like.

Same structure. Same simplicity. Same rhythm.

If you're new, stretched, or stabilising:

Stability first. Values layering second.

Direction matters more than perfection.

Compassion Pause

There will be a moment when something inside you whispers:

I should have known this sooner.

I wasted years.

I should be further ahead.

That voice isn't truth. It's human.

Midlife learning often comes with a quiet grief layer — grief for the years you were too overwhelmed to focus on yourself.

Hand on heart. One slow breath. Say:

I know better now because now is when I finally had the space to learn.

Nothing was wasted — I was surviving.

I wasn't late. I was overloaded.

I am learning at exactly the right time for me.

Write this somewhere you'll see it:

I learned exactly on time — the moment I was finally safe enough to understand.

The Quietest Kind of Wealth (Payoff Moment)

Amina was 57 when she finally opened the pension statement she'd been avoiding.

Not because she didn't care — because she was scared of how she might feel.

She made tea. Sat by the window. Let the paper rest in her hands like something fragile.

She expected shame. She expected a shock. She expected the familiar tightening in her chest — the one that always whispered: *You should have done more by now.*

But instead, something unexpected happened.

A breath.

Not relief exactly… but release. A soft unclenching inside her ribs. A moment of: *I survived more than I ever admitted.*

She didn't vow to "catch up." She didn't overhaul her finances in a wave of adrenaline.

She whispered one sentence — steady, quiet, true:

I can do this slowly.

That was her beginning.

Three years later, she wasn't "rich" in the Instagram sense. She still had responsibilities, real life, and ordinary ups and downs.

But she had something deeper:

She was no longer afraid of her future.

Her wealth wasn't the number.

Her wealth was the steadiness she built inside herself — a relationship with her future rooted in respect, not fear.

And that is the quietest kind of wealth.

Prosperisms™

These Prosperisms are the heartbeat of midlife investing — the sentences you return to when fear rises, when motivation dips, or when you need a quick reminder of your own strength.

- *Your future isn't behind you — it's waiting for you to arrive.*
- *You don't invest because you feel confident — you invest to become confident.*
- *Consistency compounds. Calm compounds faster.*
- *Slow money grows stronger than fast anxiety.*
- *Fear is a feeling, not a financial instruction.*
- *You invest in dignity as much as you invest in funds.*
- *Your wealth grows at the pace of your life — and that pace is allowed to be gentle.*
- *Late isn't late when you show up with intention.*

Key Takeaways

- "Too late" is a shame story, not a financial reality.
- Investing is ownership + time — not performance.
- Your long-term outcome is shaped mostly by time in the market and staying invested.
- The best plan is the one you can stick to calmly.
- You only need one good account, one simple fund, and one steady habit.
- Confidence comes from familiarity — five minutes a week is enough to begin.

Reflection Prompt

Safe to invest slowly:

What tiny behaviour proves I am choosing my future?

Finish the sentence:

My wealth grows at the pace of my nervous system — and right now, that pace is…

What's Next

Now we shift into work, income, and purpose: how you earn without losing yourself.

This next chapter isn't about hustling harder.

It's about earning in ways that support your energy, your boundaries, and your second act.

Turn the page when you're ready.

"I BELONG TO MY FUTURE, NOT MY PAST."

CHAPTER 9

WORK & INCOME IN MIDLIFE: EARNING WITH INTEGRITY, ENERGY, AND IDENTITY

EARNING WITHOUT ERODING YOURSELF

There comes a moment — not dramatic, not catastrophic, just quietly honest — when your relationship with work shifts.

You wake up and realise:

You no longer want to grind.

You no longer want to run on adrenaline, compliance, and decades of being "good."

You want something else:

Alignment.

Dignity.

Usefulness without depletion.

Stability without self-sacrifice.

Work that doesn't cost your nervous system more than it pays your bank account.

You're not lazy.

You're evolving.

Midlife doesn't make you less ambitious — it makes you ambitious for *the right things*.

You don't crave retirement — you crave *right work*: the kind that respects your experience, honours your energy, and doesn't require you to abandon yourself for a salary.

• • •

Tiny Real-Life Example:

Sam, 52, didn't overhaul her career.

She raised her day rate by £10 and offered one small service she actually enjoyed.

That £10 shift added £120 a month — not dramatic, but meaningful.

Small shifts protect your nervous system while strengthening your financial foundation — this is the Slow Money way.

Midlife earning is rarely transformation.

It's steady micro-adjustments that compound quietly.

This chapter is not a pep-talk to quit everything.

It's not a command to build a business.

It's not a hustle manifesto.

And it's definitely not another 'just start a side hustle!' speech — you've survived enough.

It's a guide to designing work that supports:

- your wellbeing
- your financial security
- your identity
- your capacity
- your future
- your peace

This is your second-act career — built not from urgency, but from understanding.

THE MIDLIFE WORK TURNING POINT

Something subtle happens in your 40s and 50s:

You stop trying to *become* someone.

You start trying to *be yourself* again.

The questions change.

From:

"What job should I take?"

To:

"Who am I now — and what kind of work feels good for this version of me?"

From:

"How do I get ahead?"

To:

"How do I earn without losing myself?"

From:

"What will they think of me?"

To:

"What do *I* think of me?"

This isn't collapse — it's clarity finally catching up with you.

Midlife clarity is the moment your inner voice gets louder than the external noise.

You finally recognise:

You've carried too much.

You've proved enough.

You've earned your stripes.

And you now deserve to earn without eroding your health.

This shift isn't weakness.

It's wisdom rising to the surface.

You didn't mismanage your life. You adapted to it.

And now you get to adapt again — but this time in a way that supports you too.

Your Energy Is Now Your Greatest Currency

In your 20s and 30s, work was about stamina.

Push.

Prove.

Perform.

Outwork the room.

But in midlife?

Energy becomes the real currency.

The question is no longer:

"How much can I hustle?"

It becomes:

"What can I sustain without losing myself?"

Because now:

- your body tells the truth before your mind does
- your nervous system becomes your compass

- hormones change the emotional weather
- stress hits deeper
- recovery takes longer
- meaning matters more
- boundaries aren't optional anymore

The most financially powerful midlife earners aren't the fastest.

They're the most **appropriately paced** — strategic, boundaried, energy-aware.

Your nervous system isn't a barrier to success.

It's the blueprint for sustainable success.

THE NEW MIDLIFE SUCCESS EQUATION

Success used to be:

More. Faster. Higher. Louder.

Now, success becomes:

Competence + Calm + Choice + Contribution

Not peak performance.

Not sprinting.

Not sacrificing your life for a CV line.

Midlife success is grounded:

- work you care about
- with people who respect you
- at a pace your body can hold
- for income that stabilises you
- while leaving room for your life

You don't need to look impressive.

You need to *feel supported*.

That's maturity — financially, professionally, emotionally.

Identity Shift: You're Not Starting Over — You're Starting Wiser

People call midlife career change "reinvention."

But reinvention suggests you must become someone new.

Midlife work is reclamation.

Recovering the parts of you buried under responsibility, survival, expectations, and necessity.

You're not restarting.
You're distilling.
You're not inexperienced — you're concentrated wisdom.
You haven't missed your chance.
You're refined.
Your experience is your leverage — not your liability.

"In midlife, you don't hustle for worth – you choose work that respects your nervous system."

A Story: Daniel's Tuesday Afternoon

Daniel had spent 25 years sprinting.

Early in. Late out.

Delivering. Producing. Absorbing stress like oxygen.

He wasn't unhappy — just permanently stretched. That's the danger of midlife work: it doesn't have to be miserable to be misaligned.

Then one Tuesday afternoon, sitting in a familiar boardroom with familiar faces saying familiar things, something shifted.

A quiet truth surfaced:

"I don't want this version of my life anymore."

He didn't quit.

He didn't blow up his career.

He simply… listened.

Six months later, Daniel had:

- negotiated a four-day week
- moved into a calmer department
- started a small consulting project on Fridays
- reclaimed two mornings for his health
- realised he wasn't less ambitious —

he was just ambitious for a *different* kind of life

He didn't lose anything.

He gained self-respect.

That's midlife reinvention.

Not burning it down — editing it until it fits.

Pause Here: Permission

Let this land gently:

You are allowed to choose again.

You are allowed to:

- earn more
- earn differently
- earn slowly
- earn less but live better
- pivot careers
- reduce hours
- build a second income stream
- say no to draining work
- want peace more than prestige
- want health more than hustle
- rest without earning it
- design work that honours your nervous system

You Don't Want Retirement — You Want Relief

Most midlifers don't dream of stopping work.

They dream of stopping overwhelm.

They want:

- mornings without adrenaline
- work without politics
- contribution without depletion
- colleagues who value experience
- tasks that don't require crisis-mode thinking
- time to breathe
- rest without guilt

Retirement fantasies are often rest fantasies.

You don't want to opt out of life — you want to opt out of chaos.

Who You Were at 35 Is Not the Benchmark

Your 35-year-old self had different hormones, priorities, pressures, dreams, tolerances.

That version could sprint.

This version requires pacing.

That's not decline — it's discernment.

You now carry:

- pattern recognition
- emotional intelligence
- boundaries
- clarity
- depth
- self-respect

Work must now honour:

- your nervous system
- your bandwidth
- your recovery needs
- your values
- your experience

You aren't supposed to be who you were.

You're supposed to be who you're becoming.

Energy Budget > Time Budget

In midlife, hours matter less than energy — it's your real currency now.

Ask:

- What drains me fastest?
- What restores me most?
- What tasks deplete me disproportionately?
- What pace is sustainable for years?
- Where am I over-performing out of old insecurity?
- What would work look like if it respected my actual capacity?

Success isn't endurance anymore.

Success is stewardship.

You're not fragile — you're aware.

And awareness is what turns survival patterns into sustainable earning.

• • •

Before you redesign anything, your nervous system needs clarity — not pressure, not urgency, just truth.

THE MIDLIFE WORK RESET BLUEPRINT™

STEP 1 — Awareness

The quiet noticing that something no longer fits.

Ask:

- What have I outgrown?
- What drains me?
- What excites me quietly?
- What needs to end internally before anything ends externally?

Awareness is the beginning.

STEP 2 — Adjusting the Current Life

You don't leap — you tweak.

- one boundary
- one conversation
- one shift in responsibilities
- one remote day
- one restructure of workload
- one reduction in emotional labour

Tiny edits change entire lives.

STEP 3 — Exploration Without Pressure

Curiosity, not career crisis.

- one course
- one client
- one conversation
- one shadowing day
- one skill explored
- one experiment that doesn't need to earn

This is discovery.

STEP 4 — Gentle Transition

Not burning bridges — building pathways.

- fractional work
- hybrid roles
- reducing hours
- one day a week for new income
- easy landings, not cliff jumps

STEP 5 — Integration

The moment the new identity fits.
Not rushed. Not forced.
Aligned. Sustainable. Yours.

Income Resilience in Midlife

Security now comes from **optionality**, not intensity.

Resilience =

✔ transferable skills
✔ boundaries that protect wellbeing
✔ negotiation without apologising
✔ removing single points of failure

Quiet power > constant proving.

The Midlife Income Triangle

Your most stable earning structure includes:

1 ❑ **Primary Income (humane, stabilising)**

A job that pays you without costing your health.

2 ❑ **Safety Skill (your fallback)**

Something you can always use to earn if you need to.

3 ❑ **Optional Income Stream (gentle, aligned)**

Low-pressure. Slow. Steady.

This is the Slow Money way:

Not more. Just sustainable.

OPTIONAL INCOME — THE SLOW MONEY WAY

You don't need a side hustle that devours your life.

You need a stream that hums quietly.

Examples:

✔ consulting (1 client, low pressure)
✔ fractional roles
✔ seasonal gigs
✔ micro-digital products
✔ one workshop or class
✔ advisory calls
✔ small affiliate or Pinterest income
✔ creative extras
✔ pet care / tutoring / caregiving
✔ board or committee work
✔ renting storage or tools

Slow Money rule:

If it steals your peace, it isn't wealth.

Work You Tolerated vs. Work That Honours You

Ask:

What have I tolerated because I thought I had to?
What would honour who I am now?

Honouring work feels like:

- safety
- respect
- predictability
- appropriate pace
- meaningful contribution
- enough energy left for your life

You deserve work that restores you.

Negotiation in midlife isn't confrontation — it's clarity. It's letting the role fit the human, not the other way around.

SCRIPTS FOR MIDLIFE NEGOTIATION

• Flexibility
"My best work happens when my energy is managed well. Here's a structure that supports long-term performance."

•Pay
"Given the depth of experience I bring, I'd like to align compensation with responsibility. Here's the range I'm targeting."

• Boundaries
"To maintain quality, I need clarity on priorities. Which task takes precedence?"

• Declining Tasks
"I'm at capacity with current priorities. What shall we pause or reassign if this becomes essential?"

• Proposing Reduced Hours
"I'd like to shape my role in a way that supports sustainable performance. Here's a model that benefits both sides."

• Practical Starter Script
"Hi [Name], I'd love to revisit my rate/salary. My scope has grown, and I'd love to reflect that in our agreement."

No defensiveness.
No justification.
Just grounded authority.

REFLECTION PROMPTS

- What work have I endured out of obligation?
- What work would honour the person I am now?
- What does "enough" feel like emotionally?
- Where am I overworking to avoid disappointing others?
- What if I stopped performing capability and simply was capable?
- What kind of environment allows me to stay well?

Finish:
"I don't need to prove my worth — I need to protect it."

Tiny Action

Choose ONE:

□ Remove one draining task
□ Block one weekly curiosity hour
□ Practise a negotiation script
□ Drop one guilt-based obligation
□ Explore an interest for 20 minutes
□ Rest — without earning it

Small → sustainable → powerful.

The Midlife Truth About Work

You don't hustle in midlife.

You **select.**

Refine.

Align.

Your options aren't shrinking — they're sharpening.

You have:

- higher clarity
- lower tolerance for nonsense
- wiser intuition
- stronger boundaries
- deeper desire for meaning

This isn't decline.

It's discernment.

Your Work Isn't Your Identity — It's a Tool

Work is a tool — not your worth.

You're allowed to choose new tools.

You're allowed to design tools that don't injure you.
You're allowed to outgrow old ones.
You don't fit work anymore.
Work must fit *you*.

Work Should Support Your Life — Not Replace It

Ask:

Does my work support the life I want — or consume it?

Work now must offer:

- steadiness
- emotional safety
- humane pacing
- recovery
- contribution
- flexibility
- space for health, relationships, joy

You're not designing a career.
You're designing a life.

Case Study: Mark's Second-Act Work Reset

Mark, 52, had spent three decades in a high-pressure sales role. The money was good, but the cost was hidden – burnout, health scares, and a creeping dread every Sunday night.

Instead of leaping into a brand-new career, he ran a Slow Money experiment. For six months, he negotiated a four-day week, dropped his least profitable client group, and started a tiny consulting practice on the side, using skills he already had.

The result? His income dipped slightly at first, but his energy and focus improved. Within a year, the consulting work replaced the lost salary – and his work week no longer felt like an emergency. He hadn't "burned it all down." He had reshaped it to fit the person he'd become.

"Steady is not settling. Steady is how your future self feels safe."

You Don't Need to Burn Your Life Down to Change It

Transformation is rarely dramatic.

Most reinvention looks like:

- one honest conversation
- one boundary
- reclaiming mornings
- shifting hours
- revisiting your CV quietly
- taking a small course
- trying one client
- removing one obligation
- resting long enough to hear yourself

Midlife work isn't reckless — it's respectful.

A Grounded Midlife Mantra

Say softly:

"I'm not starting again — I'm starting aligned."

That's the power of Act Two.

THE SLOW MONEY PROMISE

You no longer have to grind, chase, over-function, or sacrifice your health.

You get to:

✔ work with dignity
✔ set boundaries
✔ choose sustainable energy
✔ earn without depletion
✔ shape your role
✔ diversify calmly
✔ honour your nervous system
✔ honour your life

This is what work looks like when you stop surviving and start designing.

KEY TAKEAWAYS

• Midlife work is not about hustle — it's about alignment, dignity, and energy.

• Your earning power rises when your work stops eroding your wellbeing.

• Energy is now your greatest currency — not stamina or performance.

• Success shifts from "more, faster" to competence + calm + choice + contribution.

• You deserve income that fits who you are now, not who you were forced to be.

Reflection Prompt

• How do I want work to feel now?
• What does "enough" look like in terms of energy?
• How do I want income to support my wellbeing?
• What contribution feels meaningful?
• What am I ready to release from my old work identity?
• What one change would bring me closer to alignment?

Finish:

"I choose work that honours who I am becoming."

Tiny Action

□ Block a restorative evening
□ Edit one part of your current role
□ Remove one guilt-based task
□ Update CV/LinkedIn lightly
□ Explore a dormant interest
□ Rest

Small steps → identity shift → life shift.

You don't hustle in midlife.
You curate.
You align.

You honour yourself.
The stability you build in this chapter becomes the foundation for what comes next:

Next Chapter: Relationships, Boundaries & Shared Money

Where we explore:
- caring for others without self-erasure
- navigating shared finances gracefully
- boundaries with partners, adult children, family
- staying whole while staying connected
- protecting your emotional + financial safety simultaneously

PAUSE HERE.

Drop your shoulders.
Nothing in this chapter is urgent.
Come back into your body before we continue.

"STEADINESS IS STRENGTH."

CHAPTER 10
RELATIONSHIPS, BOUNDARIES & SHARED MONEY
MONEY IN MIDLIFE ISN'T JUST MONEY.

Money is people work in midlife.

By midlife, money shifts.

Not because the numbers change — but because the meaning does.

At 25, money feels transactional.

In your 40s, 50s, and beyond, money becomes relational.

It becomes:

- care
- duty
- resentment (the quiet kind)
- emotional labour
- invisible expectations
- the silent history of who carried what
- the pressure to be "the responsible one"
- the ache of needing help
- the pride of giving help
- the grief of feeling stretched between generations
- the longing to finally not feel alone with it all

Money becomes memory.

Money becomes story.

Money becomes identity.

And midlife is the moment all those threads pull tight — not because you've done anything wrong, but because this is the age where financial relationships collide.

Parents need more.

Children need more.

Partners need clarity.

You need boundaries.

Everyone needs something.

And you're standing in the middle, trying to hold your life together with steadiness and grace.

This chapter is the emotional backbone of your Slow Money reset.

Not the numbers. Not the spreadsheets.

The relationships behind the numbers.

Because you can budget your way out of debt and still feel drained by the weight of other people's needs.

You can raise your income and still feel like there's never enough left for you.

You can automate your future and still feel resentful, guilty, or overextended.

Midlife money work is people work.

Your boundaries, your identity, your relationships — these shape your financial life far more than any app or interest rate.

And here's the truth that changes everything:

You can care deeply without collapsing.

You can give generously without erasing your future.

You can support others without carrying the entire emotional world on your back.

This chapter shows you how.

The Midlife Money Reality

No one prepared you for this part.

You weren't taught how to:

- support adult children while planning retirement
- set boundaries with ageing parents
- talk about money lovingly with a partner
- manage a household emotionally and financially
- juggle care, guilt, duty, and exhaustion

- stop over-functioning
- stop rescuing
- stop absorbing the fallout of other people's choices
- stop becoming "the strong one" when you're tired

You learned maths in school.

You learned budgeting (maybe).

But you were rarely taught:

How to say no with dignity.

How to say yes without depletion.

How to balance love with limits.

How to include yourself in the care circle.

If nobody taught you this, that's not a failure.

That's a gap in the system.

And midlife brings those gaps to the surface at once:

- the child who needs stability
- the parent who needs support
- the partner who needs clarity
- the sibling who needs "a bit of help"
- the ex who still impacts the finances
- the friend who always leans
- the workplace that demands more

But you've spent years saying, "It's fine. I'll manage."

Until one day it isn't fine.

And you realise you managed so well, for so long, that everyone forgot you ever needed support at all.

This chapter is your permission slip to step out of that role — kindly, not abruptly — and build a steadier financial life that works for everyone, including you.

The First Boundary of Midlife

You are not the bank, the safety net, and the emotional buffer.

Midlife boundaries are not harsh.

They are kind structure — the sort that prevents bitterness from quietly building under your skin.

Here's the Slow Money truth:

You are allowed to stay generous.

You are not required to stay exhausted.

You can hold compassion and hold limits.

You can love people strongly and still say, "I can't fund that."

You can be supportive without becoming financially or emotionally porous.

Most people avoid boundaries because:

- they don't want to disappoint
- they feel responsible for everyone's stability
- they've always been "the strong one"
- they fear conflict
- they worry they'll be seen as selfish
- they're scared they'll lose closeness if they stop rescuing

But lack of boundaries creates more distance than honesty ever will.

Because over-giving often becomes:

- resentment
- fatigue
- simmering frustration
- emotional withdrawal
- quiet bitterness
- burnout

Boundaries are not walls.

They're doorways.

They allow closeness to stay possible.

Boundaries don't make love smaller.

They make love steadier.

When Helping Becomes Carrying

Here's the quiet truth many midlife households hold:

You start out helping — and somewhere along the way, you become responsible.

Helping becomes habit.

Habit becomes expectation.

Expectation becomes pressure.

Pressure becomes resentment.

And nobody notices the shift except you.

Rachel is 49. She has two teens, one ageing parent, an ex-partner with irregular child support, and a brother who "means well but is hopeless with money."

She didn't volunteer to be the financial anchor.

It just happened.

At first, she helped her mum navigate online banking.

Then the appointments.

Then the utilities.

Then the unexpected boiler repair.

She fronted it, thinking: I'll sort this later.

Later didn't come.

Her eldest asked for help with driving lessons.

Her youngest outgrew their school uniform again.

Her ex needed "a bit of flexibility this month."

Her brother called asking if she could "just spot him until payday."

Rachel sighed and said yes. She always did.

Because she was kind.

Because she was capable.

Because she felt she "should".

Then one Tuesday morning, opening her banking app, she realised:

She was supporting four adults and two teenagers — while telling herself she wasn't doing enough.

Her turning point wasn't dramatic.

It came quietly — like most midlife wisdom.

She whispered:

"If I keep rescuing everyone, I'm going to need rescuing myself."

This chapter helps you stop arriving at that point — not by withdrawing care, but by creating boundaries that protect your love and your future.

Permission to Set Boundaries

You are allowed to stop absorbing consequences that do not belong to you.

Boundaries are not rejection. They are redirection.

They say:

"I care about you."

"And I care about myself too."

"And the support I offer must be sustainable — not sacrificial."

Most people don't set boundaries until they break.

Midlife invites you to set them before then.

Because a boundary set early is a conversation.

A boundary set late is an explosion.

Choose the first.

Couples & Money

Clarity with calm.

Money conversations fail not because of numbers, but because of tone:

- blame
- fear
- pressure
- defensiveness
- unspoken resentment
- unequal emotional labour

Midlife couples thrive when money becomes a shared reality — not a secret burden carried by one person.

How to talk about money without the usual tension:

1 Start with shared goals, not past mistakes.

Try: "Where do we want to be in five years?"

Not: "Why didn't you save more?"

2 Divide the emotional load, not just the bills.

Try: "I need us to share the thinking, not just the payments."

3 Small, scheduled check-ins beat crisis conversations.

Ten minutes every fortnight is better than two hours after an argument.

4 Don't aim to match contributions — aim to match commitment.

Equality doesn't mean sameness. It means fairness.

5 Speak from vulnerability, not accusation.

Try: "I feel anxious when I don't know where we stand."

Not: "You never tell me anything."

If you're rebuilding after separation:

Midlife breakups can create financial earthquakes — practical, emotional, identity-based.

Keep this mantra:

"I will not shame my past. I will build my future deliberately."

If You Are Solo

Being single at midlife — by choice, divorce, death, or circumstance — can carry a unique emotional and financial weight.

No second income.

No shared safety net.

No built-in backup.

But here's the truth:

Solo does not mean unsupported.

Solo does not mean unsafe.

Solo does not mean you must carry everything alone.

Solo strength looks like:

- clarity over income and outgoings
- a small, steady emergency fund
- automated systems that reduce mental load
- clear boundaries with family
- a support circle (emotional, practical, social)
- a long-term plan rooted in your values

And solo midlife has a rare superpower:

You answer to yourself.

You get to rebuild without compromise.

You're allowed to choose a future that fits exactly who you are now.

Pause. Breathe. Let your shoulders drop.

Adult Children & Money

Support, not self-sacrifice.

You can support your children without financially parenting them forever.

Signs you may be carrying more than is sustainable:

- Helping with rent "until they get back on their feet"— without a clear review point
- subscriptions or ongoing costs you no longer actively choose
- convenience funding rather than true necessity
- guilt when you say no
- fear they'll struggle if you step back

- dipping into your future to subsidise their present
- emergencies that happen monthly

Adult children don't need rescuing. They need scaffolding.

Support that empowers (not enables):

- emotional support
- budgeting guidance
- encouraging an emergency fund
- clear limits on help
- timelines for support
- contributions if living at home
- conversations about independence

A healthy boundary might sound like:

"I love you. I can contribute £50, but I can't cover the full amount. Let's look at options together."

A line to remember:

"My role is support, not self-sacrifice."

Parents & Eldercare

The quiet weight you weren't prepared for.

This is the part where roles reverse — slowly, and then all at once.

You become:

- the medical advocate
- the financial organiser
- the emotional anchor
- the one who "just handles things"

Caring for parents can be both an honour and a weight.

You are not wrong for feeling both.

You are allowed to set limits.

Supporting parents does not require:

- sacrificing your pension
- hiding your exhaustion
- absorbing every crisis
- doing everything alone
- meeting every expectation

Love is not measured by how depleted you are.

A gentle line to practise:

"I'm here, and I can help — but I can't do everything."

If you're the only responsible sibling:

Being the responsible one does not mean you are the only one.

Ask directly for practical help — and if they refuse, restructure your expectations of them, not your expectations of yourself.

If you feel guilty:

Your parents didn't invest in you so you could abandon your future.

They invested so you could stand strong.

Script — when you can't afford something:

"I wish I could say yes, but I can't afford this without harming my essentials. I need to stay within what's sustainable for me right now."

Money & Guilt

If money has an emotional scent in midlife, it often smells like guilt.

Guilt for not giving enough.

Guilt for giving too much.

Guilt for wanting boundaries.

Guilt for having limits.

But guilt is not a moral compass.

Guilt is a conditioned response.

Where it often comes from:

1 Upbringing: "Good people sacrifice."

2 Comparison: everyone seems to cope better (they don't).

3 Fear: "If I say no, I'll upset them."

4 Habit: guilt becomes muscle memory.

Shift the lens:

Guilt says: "I'm failing someone."

Wisdom says: "I'm protecting everyone in the long run."

You are not responsible for funding other people's comfort at the expense of your security.

This is not selfishness. This is adulthood.

Cultural Expectations

And why your boundaries still matter.

In many cultures, interdependence is normal. Duty is woven into identity.

If saying "no" feels unthinkable, you are not wrong for feeling that.

But here is the Slow Money truth:

You cannot pour from an empty future.

A culturally gentle boundary:

"I will help in ways that protect all of us."

That means:

- not pulling from your pension
- not skipping your healthcare
- not taking on debt to support others
- not sacrificing your long-term independence

Collective strength requires your strength too.

Clean, Kind, Clear Scripts

Scripts aren't about performing — they give your nervous system a starting point when your brain goes blank.

With a partner:

- "I want us to feel secure together. Can we look at this calmly?"
- "I need us to share the thinking, not just the payments."
- "Can we have small check-ins instead of crisis conversations?"

With an adult child:

- "I love you. I'm here — and I need you to take the next step too."
- "I can support you in these ways, but not in these."

With a parent:

- "I want you supported, but I can't manage everything alone."
- "Let's make a plan so this doesn't overwhelm either of us."

With a sibling:

- "I need you to take on part of this. It can't all fall to me."
- "If you can't help financially, can you help practically?"

With yourself:

- "I can care without collapsing."
- "My future matters."
- "I am allowed to choose boundaries that keep me safe."

Reflection Prompts

• Where am I carrying more than I can sustain?

• Which responsibilities did I choose — and which did I inherit without noticing?

• What boundary would protect my peace the most right now?

• What story am I telling myself about what will happen if I set it?

• What does support look like if it doesn't rely on self-sacrifice?

• What version of me am I protecting when I set boundaries?

Finish this line (handwritten if you can):

"I deserve a financial life that doesn't depend on my exhaustion."

Tiny Steps

Choose one.

1 Have one gentle boundary conversation.

2 Say one clear "no" to a draining request.

3 Delegate one responsibility you've been carrying alone.

4 Move £10/$10 into an account labelled: "My future deserves protection."

5 Write one boundary script and practise it once.

6 Ask for help once — even something small.

Tiny scripts you can borrow:

• "I need a few days to look at my numbers before I commit to anything."

• "I can contribute £___, but I can't cover the full amount."

• "I want to help, but I can't do this alone. Let's look at options together."

The Emotional Heart of Midlife Money

You can love people deeply without losing yourself financially.

Your generosity doesn't make you weak.

Your exhaustion doesn't make you failing.

Your boundaries don't make you selfish.

Your limits don't make you unkind.

They make you sustainable.

Midlife isn't asking you to be stronger.

It's asking you to be clearer.

And clarity — spoken gently — will change everything.

This is the chapter where you reclaim the right to be supported, not just supportive.

KEY TAKEAWAYS

- Emotional labour and financial labour are deeply connected in midlife.
- Boundaries protect your energy, identity, and long-term financial safety.
- You can support others without bankrupting yourself emotionally or financially.
- Saying "no" isn't selfish — it's strategic self-respect.
- Your money life stabilises fastest when your emotional life has edges.

Tiny Action

□ Pick one bill, subscription, or regular cost and review it. Could it be paused, cancelled, or renegotiated?

Reflection Prompt — Protect Your Peace

Every time you reduce a drain on your energy or money, you honour your future self. That's prosperity too.

As we move into the next chapter, we shift from emotional boundaries into practical structure.

Where you go next isn't about hustle or urgency.

It's about building systems that support the life you're now choosing — with clarity, dignity, and ease.

Turn the page.

Your future is waiting for leadership, not fear.

“CLARITY CREATES CALM.”

CHAPTER 11

FUTURE SECURITY, LEGACY & THE EMOTIONAL RETIREMENT PLAN

THE FUTURE STOPS FEELING FAR AWAY

Your future is someone to care for.

For most of your life, the future felt like a distant country.

Retirement was an abstraction. Ageing belonged to "later." Legacy sounded like something reserved for grandparents, wealthy families, or people who "had their lives together."

Then — quietly, subtly, unmistakably — something shifts.

Not a crisis. Not a dramatic revelation.

Just a moment of truth.

A day when you catch yourself thinking:

"I want to be okay later."

"I want things to get easier, not harder."

"I want comfort — without fear."

You're not asking for extravagance.

You're asking for peace.

The kind of peace that lets you exhale.

The kind of stability that removes the background hum of anxiety.

The kind of future that feels like a soft landing, not a cliff edge.

Midlife planning isn't about preparing for old age.

It's about choosing emotional safety for the decades ahead — and building a future you can walk toward with dignity, not dread.

The goal isn't retirement.

The goal is self-trust across time.

Your nervous system is trying to picture safety, not perfection.

That's why future planning belongs to midlife more than any other season.

This Is Not a Scary Chapter

Let's be very clear from the start:

This is not a doom chapter.

This is not a "you should already have…" lecture.

This is not pressure, shame, or urgency.

This is:

- a hand on your back
- a light in the dark
- a plan you can grow into slowly
- a conversation with your future self
- grounding — not panic
- clarity — not pressure
- self-respect — not fear

Fear has never built a safe future.

Care has. Clarity has. Consistency has. Compassion has.

This chapter is an invitation — not a warning.

If you're thinking:

"I should have more saved by now."

"I wish I'd started earlier."

"What if I run out?"

"What if I become a burden?"

"I feel behind compared to everyone else."

You are not alone.

Most midlifers — even the polished, successful, outwardly composed ones — carry these thoughts privately.

But here's the truth underneath them:

You're not behind.

You're aware now — and awareness is the real beginning.

You're not catching up.

You're coming home to yourself.

Your Future Self Is Not a Stranger

A profound shift happens in midlife:

You stop seeing "future you" as a theoretical figure living in some far-off decade.

You realise:

Future you is you.

You — with softer edges.

You — with more wisdom.

You — with a body that may need more care.

You — with a heart that still wants stability, joy, and belonging.

Planning isn't an obligation.

It's companionship.

Think of this chapter as the first conversation in a lifelong friendship between present you and future you.

The Emotional Future Plan

The heart comes first.

Before we touch pensions, strategy, or paperwork, we start with emotion.

Future planning begins with feeling, not formulas.

Ask yourself:

What do I want my later life to feel like?

Write freely:

- Peace looks like…
- Comfort looks like…
- Home looks like…
- Support looks like…
- Freedom looks like…
- Connection looks like…
- Health looks like…
- Routine looks like…
- Safety looks like…

Not goals. Not numbers. Not checkboxes.

Just tone. Texture. Emotion. Vision.

Because numbers tend to follow your values.

They rarely lead them.

This is not panic planning.

This is life design.

The Three Pillars of Midlife Future Security

A calm, grounded framework.

1) Financial Stability

Calm, not complicated.

You don't need to maximise everything.

You don't need to rush.

You don't need to become a finance expert.

You need:

- enough monthly income to exhale
- a steady investing rhythm
- clearer visibility of pensions
- softened or simplified debt
- a layered emergency fund
- a light annual review
- optional future income ideas

You don't need riches.

You need predictability, dignity, and peace.

Financial stability is emotional stability.

It gives your nervous system somewhere to stand.

2) Housing & Physical Stability

Your home becomes more than shelter.

It becomes the emotional container for your future self.

Housing planning isn't about deciding today.

It's about exploring options without fear.

Ask gently:

- Do I want to stay here long-term?
- Would a simpler home bring more ease?
- Where would I feel connected?
- What environment helps me rest?
- What would "ease" look like?

You're not deciding.

You're collecting possibilities.

Preparation is the opposite of fear.

. . .

3) Emotional & Social Support

One of the biggest risks of ageing is isolation.
One of the strongest protections is connection.
Ask yourself:

- Who are my safe people?
- Where do I feel supported?
- What friendships matter?
- What community threads can I keep alive?
- What nourishes me?

Your safety net isn't made of money alone.
It's made of people — and the habits that keep you connected.

Pause: A Moment of Compassion

Place your hand on your chest.
Whisper:
"Future me, I'm coming for you — not in fear, but in honour."
You are not preparing for decline.
You are preparing for dignity.

Your Future Needs a Framework, Not a Frenzy

Most financial books begin with:
"Calculate your retirement number."
"Find the gap."
"Optimise everything."
"Beat inflation."
This book will not.
Your nervous system deserves a different entry point.
Future planning starts with:

- kindness
- clarity
- small steps
- grounded truth
- structure without overwhelm

Because you're not building a retirement plan.

You're building a life you can live in — with dignity.

As we move into pensions, wills, and long-term planning, a note: I'm speaking in broad strokes here. I can't see your full picture from where I'm sitting, so treat this chapter as a nudge toward clarity — not a replacement for personalised financial or legal advice. Use it to get informed, feel steadier, and know what questions to ask next.

THE MIDLIFE FUTURE SAFETY BASE

Your future stands on three pillars:

1 Financial Stability

2 Housing & Physical Environment Stability

3 Legal & Administrative Peace

You don't build all of this at once.

You begin shaping the pieces.

1) Financial Stability — Slow Money Style

A. Steady Contributions (Not Perfect Ones)

Your future thrives on consistency:

- pension / SIPP contributions
- ISA / 401(k) / IRA investing
- a simple investing rhythm into your 50s and 60s
- a layered emergency fund
- simplified debt
- light annual reviews
- optional future income ideas

Consistency beats intensity. Always.

B. Layered Emergency Fund

Layer 1 — Micro Cushion

Layer 2 — Soft Safety

Layer 3 — Stability Fund

You build safety through continuity, not pressure.

C. Gentle Debt Positioning

You're not eliminating everything overnight.

You're softening the edges.

D. A Transparent Money Map

Future-you needs simplicity, not mystery.

Make a list of:

- accounts
- pensions
- logins
- bills
- policies

Clarity is emotional regulation.

2) Housing Peace

Explore, don't decide.

Ask gently:

- Does this home support my future body?
- Would a smaller place feel easier?
- Where would I feel connected?

This is visioning, not committing.

3) Legal & Administrative Peace

These are not cold documents.

They are future kindness.

Your Peace Papers:

- a will
- power of attorney
- healthcare directive / wishes (where applicable)
- updated beneficiaries
- an emergency folder
- one person who knows where everything is

This is love in organised form.

Care Planning

The part nobody talks about.

Care planning isn't preparing for disaster.

It's preparing for dignity.

It is saying:

"I will not abandon the person I'll be at 65, 75, 85. I deserve to be supported — not overwhelmed."

Care planning can mean:

- anticipating future needs
- exploring support options
- reducing stress for future-you
- choosing dignity over fear
- building companionship across time

Agency is the antidote to anxiety.

If you're ageing solo

You are not unsafe.

You are not destined to struggle.

Solo ageing can be powerful, sovereign, and self-directed.

Your strength includes:

- autonomy
- clarity
- choosing your community
- alignment with your values

Solo is not a deficit.

It is a design.

Your Care Support Map

1 Your care people (who checks in, who shows up)

2 Professional support options (NHS, local services, social care, community networks, private support if needed)

3 Your preferences (not commitments):

- staying home with light support
- a smaller home
- community living
- local connection
- support with tasks

Naming your needs is grounding.

Legacy — The Gentle Definition

Legacy isn't just money.

Legacy is:

- emotional safety you pass down
- clarity you leave behind
- the boundaries you model

• the healing you create
• the stability you build
• the paperwork that spares confusion
• the stories others tell about your courage

Legacy is leaving less fear behind you than you inherited.

That alone is extraordinary.

The Future Self Ritual

Hand on chest. Say softly:

"Future me, I will not abandon you. We will age with clarity and care."

Let this settle:

"I am not running out of time.
I am stepping into my time."

Case Study: The Patel Family's Future-Ready Plan

When Priya and Sanjay hit their early fifties, they realised their money life was scattered — pensions with old employers, no will, no clear plan for helping their two adult children or ageing parents.

It felt overwhelming, so they kept putting it off.

One weekend they sat down with a notebook and did three things:

• listed every pension, savings pot, and insurance policy they could find

• booked an appointment with a solicitor to write a basic will and lasting powers of attorney

• agreed a simple family rule: any future financial help for their children would come from a specific "family fund," not random dipping into savings

None of this made them instantly "sorted."

But they both reported sleeping better.

Their future felt less like a fog and more like a path — one they were actively shaping, together.

KEY TAKEAWAYS

• Midlife planning isn't about age — it's about choosing emotional safety.
• Fear has never built a secure future; clarity, compassion, and consistency have.
• You don't need to be "ahead" — you need to be aware, and you are.
• Your future becomes calmer the moment you stop planning from panic.
• Legacy is not only wealth; legacy is the emotional imprint you leave behind.

Reflection Prompt — Future You Is Grateful

It doesn't have to be big. It just has to begin. Every small plan you make now builds future calm.

Your future is not something to fear.

Your future is someone to care for.

You don't build safety through urgency.

You build it through clarity, compassion, and small steps that honour future-you.

You are not too late.

Your timing is not a problem.

You are not starting over.

You are stepping into a second adulthood — defined by sovereignty, stability, and quiet power.

The decades ahead are not a decline.

They are an unfolding.

And you — with your Slow Money steadiness — are creating a future you can walk into with calm, dignity, and choice.

PART III — RENEW LIFE

"SAFETY BEFORE STRATEGY."

CHAPTER 12
EMOTIONAL WEALTH, SELF-WORTH & IDENTITY IN ACT TWO
THE WEALTH NO SPREADSHEET CAN MEASURE

Your money can only go where your identity allows.

There is a kind of wealth that never appears in net-worth statements.

The wealth of waking without dread.

The wealth of feeling at home in your own life.

The wealth of no longer shrinking when circumstances change.

The wealth of trusting yourself enough to rest.

The wealth of letting go of the constant performance of strength.

The wealth of not needing anyone's approval to feel legitimate.

This chapter isn't about money.

It's about the person holding the money.

Because financial peace without inner peace is just numbers sitting inside a nervous system that's overwhelmed, exhausted, or afraid.

And that is not security.

Real wealth begins when your body feels safe, your mind feels clear, and your choices feel aligned.

Money doesn't create that.

Self-respect does.

And honestly — if spreadsheets alone could fix your life, we'd all be sorted by now.

The Second-Act Identity Shift

Midlife isn't the loss of who you are.

It's the loss of who you were required to be.

For decades, you carried:

- expectations
- roles
- emotional labour
- survival strategies
- caregiving
- competence-performance
- the pressure to prove yourself

Then midlife asks a quiet question that rearranges your internal architecture:

Who am I when I'm no longer performing who I had to be?

This isn't crisis.

This is return.

Not reinvention — reclaiming.

Not starting over — stepping inward.

You aren't becoming new.

You're becoming honest.

You No Longer Need to Prove Your Worth

In your younger years, "wealth" looked like:

achievement, accumulation, efficiency, being admired, being chosen, being productive, being impressive.

But in midlife, a deeper truth emerges.

True wealth is:

- peace
- boundaries
- self-trust
- emotional capacity
- time that feels like it's actually yours
- knowing you can handle what comes
- breathing freely in your own home, work, relationships, and skin

There is maturity in reaching the place where you no longer hustle for permission.

You belong to yourself now.

And that belonging is powerful currency.

Self-Talk Shapes Your Financial Identity

You cannot build a calm financial life on a foundation of self-criticism.

Not just because it's unkind — though it is — but because shame leads to avoidance, and avoidance traps you.

Money grows in visibility.

Shame grows in shadows.

So the identity shift begins with one sentence:

"I am allowed to build wealth slowly, at a pace that honours my life."

Add what you need:

- "I am not behind — I am beginning from where I am."
- "My story doesn't disqualify me from stability."
- "I don't need perfection to be secure."
- "My pace is my strength."

This is identity work — not accounting work.

And it changes everything.

The Nervous System Contract

Your body is part of your financial life.

An overwhelmed nervous system makes money feel threatening.

A calmer nervous system makes money feel navigable.

A stressed mind avoids.

A depleted mind overspends.

A regulated mind builds steadily.

We regulate first.

Then plan.

Then act.

Most midlife money mistakes don't come from lack of knowledge.

They come from dysregulation.

When your nervous system feels safer, you naturally:

- plan instead of panic

- invest instead of avoid
- choose long-term instead of relief
- say no without guilt
- see options instead of threats

You don't need more willpower.

You need less shame.

You don't need more motivation.

You need more space.

A Micro-Story: When Stress Quietly Shapes Spending

James wasn't reckless with money. From the outside, he looked organised — bills paid, income steady, nothing dramatic.

But every time life felt overwhelming, he avoided anything to do with finances. He'd freeze at the thought of opening his banking app. He'd postpone small decisions for weeks. He'd overspend on convenience because he was exhausted, not careless.

One evening he admitted to himself:

"It's not the money that scares me. It's the feeling underneath it."

When he began regulating first — five quiet minutes before checking his accounts, grounding breaths before paying bills — his behaviour changed without force.

Not because James suddenly learned discipline.

Because his body finally felt safe enough to choose wisely.

His money didn't change.

His nervous system did.

And everything followed.

The Emotional Wealth Assets

Let's redefine "assets."

Not just pensions, equity, or investments.

Your emotional wealth includes:

- self-trust
- boundaries
- rest literacy
- energy management
- nervous system regulation

- supportive relationships
- community
- meaningful work
- the ability to say "no"
- the courage to say "yes"
- health
- hope
- self-respect

These assets compound quietly.

Every time you keep a boundary, you grow stability.

Every time you rest before collapse, you protect your future.

Every time you treat yourself as worth protecting, your financial life becomes easier to hold.

Letting Go of Old Narratives

Midlife is when you lay down stories that once protected you but now restrict you:

"I must be strong all the time."

"My needs come last."

"I have to earn rest."

"My worth is productivity."

"It's too late."

No.

Strength is sustainable pace.

Rest is a right.

Your value is inherent.

It is not too late — this is your time.

These stories were survival tools.

You outgrew them.

Now it's time to release them.

Self-Trust: The Financial Skill No One Taught You

People think financial security is built on:

discipline, motivation, knowledge, consistency, perfect behaviour.

But the real foundation is this:

Can you rely on yourself gently, consistently — even when you're

tired?

Self-trust grows through:

- repairing mistakes without self-punishment
- ten quiet minutes once a week
- not abandoning yourself when things feel heavy
- refusing to speak to yourself like an enemy
- resting without guilt

Self-trust is built in whispers, not declarations.

Reflection Prompts

Write slowly. Don't rush. Just notice.

- Where am I ready to stop performing and start being?
- What beliefs about worth am I ready to lay down?
- What emotions usually sit underneath my spending?
- What does self-respect look like in my financial choices?
- What kind of life am I building — and how do I want it to feel?

Finish:

"I choose myself without apology, gently and consistently."

Tiny Actions

Choose one:

□ Say no once this week without justifying.
□ Block one hour for rest you didn't "earn."
□ Open your banking app and breathe, not brace.
□ Replace one self-critical sentence with: "I'm learning."
□ Put £5 into a "self-trust fund."

Tiny decisions become identity.
Identity shapes behaviour.
Behaviour builds wealth.

The Wealth You Don't See

There is a kind of wealth no one applauds — but it will transform your life:

- waking without dread

- choosing rest before collapse
- trusting yourself again
- making money decisions from stability
- being on your own side
- no longer needing permission to feel legitimate

This is emotional wealth.

Financial safety means little without emotional safety.

Money supports life. Emotional wealth lets you live it.

You don't build Act Two through force.

You build it through truth.

Through self-respect.

Through inner steadiness.

Money doesn't shape your life — identity does.

And your identity is awakening: stronger, softer, steadier, wiser.

Next Chapter

Now we look at the resource beneath every financial decision: your energy.

In the next chapter, we'll explore why pace, capacity, and bandwidth matter more in midlife than any budget — and how honouring your energy creates wealth that actually lasts.

PAUSE HERE.

Drop your shoulders.

Nothing in this chapter is urgent.

Come back into your body before we continue.

“MY VALUE IS INHERENT, NOT EARNED.”

CHAPTER 13

YOUR ENERGY IS WEALTH — THE MIDLIFE BODY & FINANCIAL CAPACITY

HOW YOUR MIDLIFE BODY BECOMES THE ENGINE OF FINANCIAL CAPACITY

Your energy is the engine of your wealth.

There comes a point — somewhere between forty and sixty — when your body stops negotiating and starts telling the truth.

Not with drama.

Not with collapse.

But with a quiet, unmistakable whisper:

"We cannot live the way we used to."

Most people mistake that whisper for decline. For weakness. For something slipping away.

But it isn't loss.

It's wisdom arriving right on time.

Midlife is the season where your whole operating system updates itself. Where pace matters more than speed. Where capacity matters more than ambition. Where nervous-system safety becomes one of the most important financial tools you have.

In your twenties, wealth was energy to burn.

In your thirties, wealth was growth at any cost.

But in midlife?

Wealth becomes capacity.

Capacity to think clearly.

Capacity to rest without guilt.

Capacity to make decisions from calm instead of adrenaline.

Capacity to set boundaries without apology.

Capacity to build systems that protect you, instead of draining you.

Money does not come from effort alone. It comes from energy, clarity, regulation, recovery, and resilience.

And all of that lives in your body — not your spreadsheets, not your calendar, not another round of self-pressure disguised as motivation.

Midlife isn't the end of energy. It's the evolution of it.

Not "I can't."

But "I choose differently now."

Not "I'm slowing down."

But "I'm becoming powerful in a new way."

Not "I've lost my edge."

But "I've lost my tolerance for depletion — and that is strength."

Your body is not working against you. It is trying to protect you from a version of life you've outgrown.

This chapter honours that shift.

Because your energy isn't a side note in your financial life — it is the engine of your wealth.

Your Nervous System Is Part of Your Financial Plan

Your financial life isn't shaped only by income, interest rates, or investment decisions. It is shaped — quietly but powerfully — by your nervous system.

Stress changes how you spend.

Fatigue changes how you plan.

Burnout changes your motivation.

Hormones change your cognition.

Inflammation changes your mood.

Sleep changes your judgment.

Loss changes your identity.

Caregiving changes your bandwidth.

Grief changes your priorities.

If you've felt inconsistent, scattered, or "not yourself," there is nothing wrong with you.

You're not undisciplined.

You're not "failing to get it together."

You're not losing ground while everyone else speeds ahead.

You're human — and you are living through one of the most demanding emotional, physical, and mental seasons of your life.

When you were younger, adrenaline was fuel.

In midlife, adrenaline becomes a tax — a cost your body can no longer afford.

Cortisol becomes expensive.

Clarity becomes currency.

Rest becomes return on investment.

This isn't decline. This is evolution.

Your body is saying:

"We are no longer doing life on survival mode — we are doing it on sustainability."

As you learned in the Calm Money chapter, dysregulation shrinks options. Regulation widens them. Midlife magnifies that effect.

Why Health Belongs in a Money Book

Traditional finance books pretend the body doesn't exist — as if decisions happen in a vacuum, as if you can budget your way out of burnout or spreadsheet your way through exhaustion.

But here's the truth you've lived:

Money is emotional.

Money is physical.

Money is nervous-system work.

When your mind is overloaded, budgeting means nothing.

When you're overwhelmed, debt plans collapse.

When you're depleted, spending becomes soothing instead of intentional.

When you're stressed, shame tricks you into avoidance.

Clarity requires capacity.

Planning requires presence.

Wealth grows in regulation — not adrenaline.

Shame says, "Try harder."

Your body says, "Slow down so you can think again."

That's why health belongs in a money book — not as a side chapter, not as "extra advice," but as a fundamental pillar, as real and essential as pensions, savings, or index funds.

Your capacity is your capital.

Every time you sleep well, your decision-making improves.

Every time you nourish yourself, panic softens.

Every time you rest, clarity returns.

Every time you regulate, your financial progress becomes sustainable.

Rest is not indulgence.

Rest is not procrastination.

Rest is not a luxury.

Rest is a financial strategy.

Your financial future is shaped by the health of the person steering it.

And that person deserves care — not criticism.

Quick note: this chapter isn't medical advice. If something feels worrying or unusual, speak with a healthcare professional. This chapter is here to help you make sense of your experience — not diagnose it.

Midlife Brain: You're Not Forgetful — You're Overloaded

One of the most unsettling parts of midlife is how your brain behaves.

Words disappear mid-sentence.

You walk into a room and forget why.

Your frustration tolerance shrinks.

Multitasking becomes harder.

Social interactions drain you more deeply.

Decision-making takes longer.

This is not personal failure.

And for many people, it isn't "decline" — it's overload.

You are carrying more life than ever before — often invisibly. Your brain isn't malfunctioning. It is prioritising survival and energy conservation after years of responsibility, stress, and emotional labour.

Your younger self could override everything with adrenaline. Your midlife self often can't — not because you are weaker, but because your brain has learned the truth:

"Sprinting is no longer sustainable."

The answer isn't "try harder."

The answer is: *What does my brain need?*

Support.
Structure.
Space between tasks.
Less noise.
More recovery.
Gentler expectations.

When you support your brain instead of shaming it, clarity returns far more easily than you expect.

Case Studies: When Energy Returns, Wealth Follows

Midlife financial change rarely begins with a budget. It begins with a body reaching its threshold — and a life that finally needs to be lived differently.

Case Study 1: Sarah, 52

Two teenagers. An ageing mother. A demanding senior role. Perimenopause arriving with unpredictable force.

Sarah didn't "lose motivation" — she lost bandwidth.

She began with capacity, not pressure:

- a simple sleep ritual
- a one-hour Sunday reset
- automatic bill payments
- saving £10/week
- sharing one responsibility at home

Six months later:

- a small emergency buffer
- regular tiny investments
- a clearer head
- peace instead of panic

Her wealth didn't grow because she hustled harder. It grew because her energy returned.

Case Study 2: Mark, 56

Mark was "the reliable one." The person who absorbed everything. Then came exhaustion that weekends couldn't fix.

His clarity returned when he rebuilt foundations:

- a protein-rich breakfast
- ten minutes of daylight walking
- a saner calendar

- a five-minute weekly money check-in
- a standing order to savings

He wasn't broken. He was tired.

And once steadier, his money followed his clarity.

These stories are not anomalies. They are midlife patterns.

The Three Wealth Skills of Midlife

Midlife wealth is built on three skills younger versions of you didn't understand — but older versions of you depend on:

1. Pacing

Slow isn't stuck. Slow is strategic. Slow compounds.

This is nervous-system intelligence, not decline.

2. Boundaries

In youth, you may have survived by saying yes.

In midlife, boundaries become wealth protection.

Every "Not right now," "That doesn't work for me," "I can't carry that," creates more stability than any budgeting hack.

3. Recovery

Rest isn't a reward. It's fuel.

Your younger self pushed through exhaustion.

Your midlife self builds through restoration.

Tiny Midlife Wealth Habits

Choose one:

- Ten-minute walk before any money task
- Phone down one hour before bed
- One protected morning each week
- A warm Sunday night planning ritual
- One white-space day each month
- Protein + water before coffee
- No phone in the bedroom
- A "calm money" playlist

Small actions. Big stability.

Scripts for Low-Energy Days

When your brain says, "I can't," say:

"I will choose one thing and postpone the rest."

When motivation disappears, say:

"Motivation was never the plan — systems are."

When shame appears, say:

"I am late to nothing."

When panic rises, say:

"Urgency is not the plan — clarity is."

When overwhelm rises, say:

"One breath. One task. One tiny money act."

These scripts keep you moving, gently.

The Gentle Midlife Support Checklist

Not rules — support.

- Sleep is sacred
- Protein + plants
- Movement without punishment
- Morning light
- Less news, less noise
- Ask for help sooner
- Joy as medicine
- Walk with a friend instead of scrolling
- Support > self-attack
- Book the appointment you've delayed

Your capacity is worth protecting.

KEY TAKEAWAYS

- Your bandwidth is a financial asset.
- Midlife requires energy-led planning, not pressure-led pushing.
- Honouring your pace creates results that last.
- Financial capacity rises when your nervous system feels safer.
- Your body is not the problem — it's the engine you build wealth with.

Tiny Action

□ Write down one decision that drained you. Then write down one support or system you could add next time.

Reflection Prompts

- What is draining me that didn't used to?
  - Where does my body say "not this pace"?
  - What would financial progress look like if gentleness led?
  - What am I ready to release?
  - What can I ask for help with?
  - What does energy wealth mean to me now?

Finish:

"I do not earn my safety by pushing — I build it by honouring my body."

Your younger self built on adrenaline. Your next self builds on awareness.

This is not decline. This is upgrade.

You are not running out of time. You are learning to use it better.

Your energy is not a side topic. It is the engine of your wealth. You protect it now because you intend to live long enough to enjoy everything you're building.

Slow. Steady. Strong.

This is midlife money wisdom.

Now that you understand the engine of wealth — your capacity — we move into the systems that let your life run with less effort and more clarity.

This is where the internal work meets the external tools.

Where your nervous system and your money plan finally work together.

Let's step into the next chapter with steadiness.

Your future is ready for structure.

"SLOW MONEY. DEEP LIFE."

CHAPTER 14
YOUR SLOW WEALTH LIFE FRAMEWORK
DAILY, WEEKLY & MONTHLY RITUALS FOR CALM, SUSTAINABLE GROWTH

Rituals that protect your peace.

Perfection was never the destination — it was never the assignment.

You were never designed to sprint endlessly, perform constantly, or chase a version of life that keeps moving the goalpost. You were never meant to stretch yourself thinner, take on more, or uphold a pace your nervous system can't sustain.

The goal has always been steadiness — a financial life that feels like an exhale, a rhythm your body can actually live inside, a way of moving through money that softens panic, quiets shame, and replaces both with ease, predictability, and peace.

This chapter is your **Slow Wealth Life Framework**™.

Not strict routines.

Not performance disguised as productivity.

Not hustle dressed up as self-improvement.

These are your daily, weekly, monthly, seasonal, and annual tethers — the practices that keep you anchored when life becomes noisy, busy, beautiful, chaotic, or uncertain.

Your confidence won't come from mastering everything. It will come from knowing the next gentle step — and taking it calmly.

THE SLOW WEALTH FLOW

Imagine your financial life as a soft, predictable cycle — one that feels lived, not forced:

Step 1 — Check in with your energy

Your body leads; money follows. Presence before planning.

Step 2 — Spend and earn with intention

Alignment over intensity — always. Each decision asks:

"Does this support the life I'm building?"

Step 3 — Allocate calmly

Automate what you can. Simplify what you can't.

Systems carry what your energy can't.

Your systems shouldn't demand perfection — they should protect your capacity.

Step 4 — Review at the right pace

Not obsessively. Not avoidantly. Just rhythmically.

Step 5 — Rest, recalibrate, repeat

Recovery is strategy. Stability is wealth.

You are the system — and the system is only strong when you are supported.

Money sits inside your life. Not the other way around.

A STORY: When Routine Became Relief

Louise, 54, was brilliant at managing everyone else's life — family calendars, work commitments, household admin, a million moving pieces she somehow kept spinning.

But her own money? Chaotic.

Not because she didn't care — but because she never had the bandwidth to look at it calmly.

Every time she "tried to get organised," she burned out within a week.

One day, instead of creating another all-or-nothing system, she asked:

"What is the smallest routine I can actually live inside?"

She started with five minutes a day. A glance at her accounts. One tiny savings transfer. A gentle sentence to herself:

"I am tending to my life."

Six months later:

- Her overdraft was gone
- She had a soft £600 buffer
- She felt calmer, clearer, more grounded
- Money no longer felt like shame — it felt like support

Her wealth didn't grow because she overhauled her life.

It grew because she stopped overwhelming herself.

Tiny rhythms. Gentle consistency.

This is Slow Wealth taking root.

DAILY RITUALS

2–5 minutes

These are the tiny moves that keep your money life gently in motion — even on tired days.

- Look at your spending once — not on an anxious loop
- Pause before a purchase
- Ask: "Does this choice support my peace?"

Calm choices compound faster than pressured ones.

Choose one self-kindness line:

- "I'm building safety, not speed."
- "I'm allowed to take this slowly."
- "Future me will feel safe because of today's softness."

Your mind responds to reassurance more than pressure.

Daily gentleness rewires your financial identity faster than discipline ever could.

WEEKLY RITUALS

10–20 minutes

Once a week, give your money fifteen honest minutes — just enough to stay in relationship with it.

Your Slow Wealth Weekly: connected, not pressured.

- Check balances
- Confirm automations ran
- Move one tiny amount into savings or investing
- Remove one digital or mental stressor

- Ask: "Did I honour my energy this week?"

The numbers matter.

But identity is what keeps them growing.

MONTHLY RITUALS

Once a month, zoom out. Check the bigger picture and make one deliberate adjustment.

- Review spending without self-attack
- Top up sinking funds
- Increase automations by £5–£10 if possible
- Review subscriptions
- Name one decision you're proud of

Reflect:

- "What gave me life this month?"
- "What quietly drained me?"

Awareness is what turns patterns into choices.

Money responds to awareness, not force.

QUARTERLY RITUALS

Every quarter, pause to check your direction — not to judge yourself, but to make sure your money life still matches your season.

Seasonal Slow Wealth reflections:

- Review pensions / retirement accounts / tax-advantaged savings
- Revisit goals for relevance, not obligation
- Ask: "What season am I in right now?"

Growth. Stabilisation. Rest. Recovery. Transition.

Check pensions and investments without making unnecessary changes — long-term strategies rarely need constant adjusting.

If the account names in this book don't match the ones in your country, simply map them to your local equivalents. Always check current rules and tax treatment in your region before changing or opening accounts.

Your financial plan should adapt to your season — never to your fear.

ANNUAL RITUALS

Once a year, step back and look at the whole landscape of your life — a gentle reset that realigns your plans, priorities, and pace for the path ahead.

Your calm review day.

A ritual — not a reckoning.

- Review your full financial snapshot
- Update your will and beneficiaries
- Review protection plans
- Review income and career direction
- Adjust investments only if needed
- Set one emotional goal and one financial goal
- Gratitude list: "What did I build, preserve, survive, soften, learn, or reclaim?"

This isn't punishment.

This is witnessing your growth.

Reviewing your year through compassion — not criticism — is what keeps consistency alive.

THE SLOW WEALTH PLANNER QUESTIONS

Use these whenever you feel off track:

- What am I actually building toward?
- How do I want money to feel in my life?
- What pace supports my nervous system?
- What tiny step honours my future this month?
- What boundary protects my energy?
- What kind of life am I designing?

The life comes first.

The numbers follow.

YOUR NON-NEGOTIABLES LIST

Midlife gives you permission to draw lines that protect your pace and your peace.

Examples:

- No sacrificing health for income
- No shame spirals
- No chasing what drains me
- No shrinking to stay acceptable
- No rushing to prove anything
- No abandoning future-me
- No guilt for resting
- No apologising for boundaries

Boundaries are wealth.

KEY TAKEAWAYS

- Consistency is built in micro-moments, not massive effort.
- Rituals remove chaos and replace it with calm, predictable structure.
- You don't need motivation — you need gentle repetition.
- Money steadiness comes from staying in relationship with your numbers.
- These rituals anchor your identity as a calm, capable steward of your future.

Tiny Action — Slow Wealth Edition

Choose one this week:

□ Check your accounts for 30 seconds — no judgment

□ Add £/$1–5 to savings (identity over amount)

□ Delete one financial stressor (an email, app, tab)

□ Do one money task with calm music playing

□ Walk for five minutes before a money decision

□ Say: "I build wealth at my pace."

□ Review one automation

□ Do one money task slowly on purpose — as proof urgency isn't required

□ Honour one boundary that protects your energy

Tiny actions build long-term identity.

THE REFLECTION RITUAL — The Quiet Review

Sit somewhere comfortable.

Place one hand on your chest, one on your stomach.

Breathe slowly.

Ask yourself:

- Where did I move gently this month?
- What did I protect?
- What did I release?
- What felt aligned?
- What would future-me want me to continue?
- What tiny next step feels kind and possible?

Then repeat:

"My life grows stronger when I go slowly."

"My consistency is enough."

"I'm building stability, not speed."

"I trust my pace."

Let your shoulders soften.

You are doing beautifully.

Reflection Prompt — You're Building Rhythm

The goal isn't speed. The goal is a life that flows at your pace.

You are not behind when you're aligned.

You've built rhythm. You've shaped structure. But real life doesn't stay still.

Midlife comes with texture — curveballs, seasons, pauses, and unexpected changes that don't fit neatly inside any plan. In the next chapter, we explore what happens when life shifts under your feet — and how to stay steady, resourced, and self-trusting even when the path changes.

You don't need perfection to build wealth.

You need a plan that bends with your life — not one that breaks your spirit.

"I RISE DIFFERENTLY NOW."

CHAPTER 15
THE TRUTH ABOUT MIDLIFE CRISES
WHY YOUR INTERRUPTIONS ARE TURNING POINTS — NOT FAILURES

When life interrupts — and you rebuild with steadiness.

Midlife isn't failure.

Midlife is data — and often, tenderness.

There comes a moment — sometimes loud, sometimes unbearably quiet — when life interrupts your rhythm. Not to punish you. Not to expose you. But to redirect you toward a life that finally matches your truth.

You didn't plan for:

- redundancy
- illness or deep fatigue
- divorce or quiet disconnection
- parenting challenges you never imagined
- ageing parents needing new levels of support
- financial shocks arriving out of nowhere
- unexpected bills
- emotional burnout
- the panic of "How did I get here?"
- the pressure of being everyone's safety net
- the heaviness of surviving instead of optimising
- the weight of being strong for too long

If any part of you whispers, *"I should be further ahead…"*

Let this land:

You didn't fall behind. You lived.

You cared for people. You carried homes. You held emotional weight no one saw. You adapted under pressure. You survived storms you never expected to walk through.

That is not failure. That is the cost of caring.

That is resilience disguised as exhaustion — and exhaustion is not proof you're behind. It's proof you're human.

Now, we rebuild — not from shame, but from truth.

Micro-Story: When David Hit the Wall

David, 51, didn't realise he was burning out until the day he sat in his car after work and couldn't turn the key.

Nothing dramatic had happened. He was simply… finished.

He wasn't lazy. He wasn't failing. He was overloaded — carrying a job, a divorce, a mortgage, two teenagers, and an ageing parent on his back.

His crisis wasn't collapse.

It was clarity:

"I can't keep living at this pace."

That whisper wasn't defeat.

It was data — the first sign that his next chapter needed a different kind of strength.

THE MYTH OF THE STRAIGHT LINE

We grow up believing life arrives in an orderly sequence:

Study → Work → Progress → Save → Settle → Grow → Retire → Peace.

A neat trajectory. A predictable climb. A sensible, linear path.

And then… real life arrives.

Real life is not a straight line. It is:

- a curve
- a loop
- a detour
- a collapse followed by a rise
- a rise followed by stillness

- stillness followed by a chapter you never saw coming

No one in midlife gets here untouched.

Everyone you think is "ahead" has a chapter they don't talk about:

- the redundancy that shattered their confidence
- savings wiped out in a divorce
- the illness that changed everything
- the year they couldn't think clearly
- the burnout hidden under a smile
- becoming a caregiver overnight
- the emergency that drained the buffer
- the fear tucked under functioning

People don't get ahead because nothing broke.

They get ahead because they rebuilt.

If someone looks collected, it doesn't mean they never cracked. It means they patched themselves together with grace and grit.

You are not weak for needing to rebuild.

You are profoundly human.

Midlife is not the season where you fall behind.

It is the season where you finally realise: everyone is carrying something.

You're living a human story — not a highlight reel.

And rebuilding is not failure.

Rebuilding is adulthood in its highest form.

YOUR RESET PHILOSOPHY

When life shifts, you don't fall apart.

You reset.

Resets aren't collapses — they are recalibrations. Moments where life whispers:

"This pace can't come with you into the next season."

A reset is not punishment. It's re-orientation. A purposeful pause. A soft clearing of the emotional table so you can choose with clarity.

And here's the part nobody says out loud:

Most midlife resets begin in exhaustion, not inspiration.

So your philosophy must be built on compassion, not critique. Kindness, not urgency. Nervous-system safety, not hustle.

A Slow Money Midlife Reset™ looks like:

• **Lower pressure** — you stabilise before you optimise

• **Reduced speed** — you stop sprinting; you let your breath catch up

• **Tighter focus** — one priority at a time

• **Essential spending only** — not forever; just until survival mode softens

• **Simplified investing** — tiny, consistent deposits; consistency beats intensity

• **Emotional kindness** — less self-attack, more self-permission

• **Returning to basics** — sleep, hydration, calm mornings, two admin tasks, your weekly wealth ritual

• **Rebuilding trust** — small promises kept; confidence returning slowly, steadily, wisely

A reset is not collapse.

A reset is regeneration.

Before you begin, take one breath.

You're not fixing your life — you're steadying yourself.

WHEN CRISIS HITS: YOUR RESET ANCHOR SEQUENCE

This is your Slow Money "break glass in case of emergency" plan. Follow it gently, in order.

1 Stabilise Essentials

Home, utilities, food, transport.

2 Reduce Outgoings to Minimum

Not deprivation — stabilisation.

3 Maintain One Tiny Savings Habit

£5/£10 a week or month. Identity over amount:

"I am someone who still saves, even in crisis."

4 Avoid Shame-Fuelled Decisions

Shame makes you reactive. Reactiveness creates regret. Pause first. Decide later.

5 Regulate Before You React

Your body must be calm enough to choose wisely.

6 Calm First. Choices Second. Always.

You don't force momentum in crisis. You preserve capacity.

When strength returns, momentum follows.

. . .

WHY RESETS WORK

Some crises are about money.

Many are about what money is sitting *inside*:

- depletion
- overwhelm
- burnout
- grief
- trauma responses
- cognitive fatigue
- dysregulation
- identity strain

This is why "budget better" often fails in midlife.

You don't need more discipline.

You need more capacity.

Resets rebuild capacity so you can meet your life with clarity again.

MICRO-RECOVERY VS. REINVENTION

Culture worships reinvention:

Quit everything. Move abroad. Start fresh. Be a phoenix.

Real midlife recovery is quieter: gentle, paced, sustainable, humane.

Reinvention says: "Come back stronger."

Slow Money says: "Come back steadier."

Midlife isn't asking for force.

It's asking for rhythm.

WHAT CRISIS REALLY LOOKS LIKE

Crisis recovery often looks like:

- answering one difficult email
- paying one overdue bill
- opening your bank app after months
- making one meal at home

- asking for help
- moving £5 into savings
- choosing rest instead of panic
- refusing to collapse into shame
- believing in a future you can't yet see

This is progress.
This is strength.
This is resilience — midlife edition.

A Story: The Week Grace Began Again

Grace, 54, wasn't avoiding money because she was careless.

She was avoiding it because she was tired — body-tired, brain-tired, soul-tired.

She told herself she needed a "fresh start." But the idea of a fresh start made her shut down even more.

So she chose micro-recovery:

Day 1 — Opened one envelope
Day 2 — Checked one balance
Day 3 — Deleted 147 old emails
Day 4 — Set up a £10 weekly transfer
Day 5 — Told her sister the truth
Day 6 — Took a guilt-free nap
Day 7 — Logged into her pension for the first time in a year

None of it was dramatic.
All of it was powerful.
Thirty days later, she wasn't "fixed."
But she was regulated, clearer, and hopeful again.
Micro-recovery didn't save her life.
It restored her capacity to save herself.

THE MIDLIFE RESET LADDER™

A calm, practical, nervous-system-aware path back to stability.

You climb slowly.
You don't skip rungs.
You don't pressure yourself.

You ascend at the pace your body can carry — not the pace your old life demanded.

Rung 1 — Stabilise (Essentials Only)

"What keeps me safe today?"

Rung 2 — Create One Tiny Habit

One micro-action. Identity over intensity.

Rung 3 — Reduce Noise

You can't hear your truth through the roar of the world.

Rung 4 — Ask for Support

Support isn't weakness. It is sustainability.

Rung 5 — Strengthen Systems Slowly

Structure is safety.

Rung 6 — Invest Again Gradually

Peace before performance.

Rung 7 — Rebuild Self-Belief

The real top of the ladder.

You'll climb this ladder many times.

That isn't regression — it's being human.

IF YOU ARE STARTING AGAIN (AGE 40–65+)

There is a moment in midlife when you look at your finances and think:

"I am starting again… and I didn't expect to be."

Let this anchor you:

Starting again in midlife is not failure.

It is evolution.

Most people start again in midlife — they just don't admit it.

You're not beginning at zero.

You're beginning with wisdom your younger self never had.

Experience compounds faster than money ever will.

THE MIDLIFE COMEBACK BLUEPRINT

A slow, calm, repeatable plan:

1 Stabilise before you optimise

2 Build tiny wins

3 Simplify everything

4 Automate essentials
5 Prioritise consistency over amount
6 Increase gently
7 Protect peace as fiercely as you protect money
Burnout steals more wealth than any low income.

IF YOUR STARTING POINT INCLUDES...

Fear

Fear isn't failure — it's awareness.

Script: "I'm building safety, not wealth today."

Debt

Debt does not disqualify you. Debt is often a symptom of care.

You will clear it using structure — with **Snowball Plus™** as your anchor.

No Savings

You're not starting with nothing. You're starting with clarity, courage, and intention.

Burnout

Burnout is a receipt of everything you carried.

Your next chapter will be built on pacing, not pressure.

Shame

You did the best you could with the knowledge, support, and capacity you had.

Hope

The spark is data. It's your nervous system softening.

KEY TAKEAWAYS

- Midlife crises are not collapses — they're interruptions that reveal truth.
- Everyone you admire rebuilt themselves; struggle is universal, not personal failure.
- You didn't fall behind — you lived, you cared, you carried more than most.
- Resilience often looks like exhaustion — and exhaustion is not a moral failure.
- Midlife isn't a crisis — it's a recalibration toward your real life.

. . .

Tiny Actions for Beginning Again

Choose one:

□ Move £5 into savings
□ Face one bill
□ Log into one account
□ Set one boundary
□ Drink water before money tasks
□ Rest for one hour
□ Write one hope for future you
□ Delete one stressor
□ Tell someone: "I'm rebuilding."

Tiny actions build identity.

Identity builds stability.

Stability builds wealth.

THE CLOSING TRUTH

Starting again isn't a setback.

It's a rite of passage.

The version of you reading this now is wiser, steadier, stronger, and more emotionally literate than any younger version you've ever been.

Starting again in midlife is not failure — it's initiation.

And you are ready.

You've moved through crisis, clarity, and reset. You've stabilised. You've softened the panic. You've remembered your strength.

Now you step into a different phase — your self-design era. Not survival mode. Not firefighting. Not "fixing."

The next chapter is intentional life-building — the blueprint for your second act. A life built not from pressure, but from truth.

Let's begin.

“I SHARPEN, I DON’T SHRINK.”

CHAPTER 16

YOUR SECOND-ACT IDENTITY + LIFE BLUEPRINT

RECLAIMING THE QUALITIES YOU THOUGHT YOU'D LOST

You don't shrink. You come into focus.

There's a myth that the first half of life is for building and the second half is for shrinking.

No.

The first half is for becoming functional in the world.

The second half is for becoming free in it.

Your younger years demanded performance — career building, family building, identity building, holding-it-all-together building.

Your second act demands alignment.

This is the turning point where something in you quietly shifts from asking:

"Who must I be to keep everything going?"

to

"Who am I now that I no longer owe anyone a performance?"

You're not chasing anymore — you're choosing.

You're not proving anymore — you're expressing.

You're not trying to fit a shape — you're finally taking your true one.

Midlife isn't winding down.

It's refining — the way wisdom settles into your bones.

You don't shrink here.

You come into focus.

You aren't starting over — you're returning.

Not reinvention. Reclaiming.

Because the parts of you rising now?

They aren't new.

They're the parts you buried under responsibility, productivity, and being the reliable one for everyone else.

And now they're knocking — quietly, but insistently.

What Second Adulthood Looks Like in Real Life

Not dramatic reinventions.

Small, practical returns.

It looks like:

- you stop saying yes out of obligation
- you stop rescuing people at the cost of your own stability
- you choose work that matches your energy — not your old identity
- you protect your capacity with clearer boundaries, slower mornings, steadier pacing
- you make decisions that honour who you are now, not who you used to perform

Second adulthood isn't about becoming someone new.

It's about finally living as the person you've always been underneath the noise.

Micro-Story: When Leo Finally Looked Up

Leo, 49, spent decades being "the dependable one" — the one who solved everything, needed nothing, and ran on silent competence.

Then one Saturday morning, parked outside the supermarket, he felt it:

not panic, not burnout — just a quiet truth.

"I don't want to live like this anymore."

He didn't quit his job or change his life overnight.

He simply stopped abandoning himself.

Smaller days. Slower mornings. Clearer boundaries.

Work that matched his energy instead of his old identity.

He didn't reinvent.

He returned — and returning changed everything.

. . .

Act Two Isn't Reinvention — It's Return

People talk about "reinventing yourself" in midlife as if you need to become someone entirely different.

But reinvention is often code for:

"I've been carrying so much for so long that parts of me slipped out of sight."

Act Two isn't about creating a brand-new identity.

It's about unearthing the original one.

Under the layers — the roles, the pressure, the over-giving, the emotional labour — you'll find the you that existed before life became a series of obligations:

- the quiet creative spark
- the curiosity
- the humour
- the gentleness
- the desire for meaning without martyrdom
- the ambition that's no longer frantic — but elegant
- the joy you postponed because life demanded seriousness
- the values you swallowed to "keep the peace"
- the dreams you delayed because someone always needed you first

This chapter is your permission slip to bring those parts home.

You don't need a new life.

You need a true life — one that matches your season, your wisdom, your clarity, your capacity.

Act Two isn't a crisis.

It's a remembering.

The Survival Identity vs. The Real You

Look at the first half of your life with compassion.

You were shaped by:

- responsibility
- financial pressure
- caregiving

- cultural expectations
- the need to stay afloat
- the pressure to perform, provide, and hold things together

You became who you needed to be for the season you were in.
But seasons change.
A survival identity is brilliant for surviving.
It isn't meant to be carried forever.
The question now isn't:
"How do I become more?"
It's:
"How do I become myself again?"
Self-return is the quiet revolution of midlife.

Purpose in Midlife Is Quieter — and Wiser

Purpose in your twenties is loud: titles, goals, proving, being seen.

Purpose in midlife is grounded. It sounds like:

"I want mornings that feel like my life, not my punishment."

"I want clarity, not chaos."

"I want to contribute — but I will not collapse to do it."

"I want work that doesn't steal my health."

"I want the time I have left to feel like it belongs to me."

Purpose isn't a mission statement.

It's a direction — steady, human, sustainable.

Your purpose now isn't what impresses others.

It's what steadies you.

The Second-Act Compass

Act Two decisions are guided by deeper values — not external pressure.

These are your new north stars:

Self-Respect — I no longer abandon myself to be approved of.

Simplicity — I choose clarity over chaos.

Health — my body and nervous system are not negotiable.

Contribution — I give where it's aligned, not where I feel obligated.

Joy — small joys daily; larger ones planned.

Autonomy — I build choices: financial, emotional, lifestyle.

Connection — relationships that nourish rather than drain.

If your life honours these, you are wealthy — regardless of your portfolio.

This isn't fluff.

This is Slow Money psychology:

Financial stability grows best inside emotional stability.

Purpose grows best inside simplicity.

Clarity grows best inside calm.

Your new compass isn't ambition.

It's alignment.

The Pace of Act Two

In your first act, speed got rewarded.

In your second act, speed breaks things.

This stage rewards:

- consistency over intensity
- depth over volume
- intention over impression
- pacing over grinding
- clarity over noise
- "enough" over "more"
- rest over martyrdom
- capacity over adrenaline
- joy over achievement

The question is no longer:

"How fast can I go?"

It becomes:

"How far can I go without losing myself?"

You're not building for applause anymore.

You're building for longevity. For dignity. For a life you can actually live inside.

This is slow success — the kind that lasts.

Design Your Days, Not Your Decade

Act Two isn't a five-year plan.

It's a Tuesday plan.

Big visions often overwhelm.

Daily rhythms transform.

Ask yourself:

- What does a nourishing morning look like now?
- What work rhythm supports my mind and body?
- How much quiet do I need to stay sane?
- Where does joy live in my week — not someday, *this week*?
- What drains me unnecessarily?
- What feels like relief?
- What feels like alignment?

A life is built from mornings, meals, habits, boundaries, money routines, movement, rest, joy, simplicity, systems — and self-respect.

Design your day, and your identity follows.

Design your identity, and your future follows.

THE SECOND-ACT LIFE BLUEPRINT

This blueprint isn't a goal sheet.

It's a gentle map back to yourself.

1) How I Want to Feel in My Second Act

Choose 3–5:

□ Calm □ Grounded □ Safe □ Creative □ Connected

□ Energised □ Respected □ Peaceful □ Capable □ Free

These aren't luxuries.

They're your internal financial metrics.

2) Where I Want to Grow Now

Choose what resonates — not what looks impressive:

□ Financial confidence

□ Health + vitality

□ Boundaries

□ Emotional steadiness

□ Creativity + play

□ Community

□ Rest

□ Purposeful work

□ Joy tolerance (allowing yourself to feel good without guilt)

□ A gentle second income stream

□ Self-respect

□ Peace

Growth doesn't need to be loud.

It needs to be aligned.

3) What I'm Releasing in Act Two

Act Two requires subtraction as much as addition:

□ Rushing

□ Proving

□ People-pleasing

□ Emotional over-functioning

□ Hustle identity

□ Financial martyrdom

□ Perfection pressure

□ Doing everything alone

□ Shame about the past

□ Performing capability

□ Overspending from exhaustion

□ Carrying responsibilities that aren't mine

Releasing these isn't selfish.

It's self-protection — and self-protection strengthens your financial future.

4) What I Want Life to Look Like Now

Not fantasy-life — functional, soulful life:

Mornings: What pace regulates me?

Work: How much, what kind, what intensity — with what boundaries?

Relationships: Who nourishes me? Who drains me? What needs updating?

Health: What does care look like in this season?

Money: What does "enough" mean now — and what systems support it?

Joy: Where does joy live in my week — *this week*?
Blueprints don't demand big changes.
They clarify direction.

Micro-Story: Chris, 54 — The Quiet Return

Chris assumed Act Two meant slowing down.

It didn't. It meant waking up.

He didn't quit his job.

He didn't move abroad.

He didn't start a business overnight.

He made one internal shift:

He stopped chasing and started choosing.

He restructured his week. Took morning walks instead of scrolling. Mentored younger colleagues. Built a small consulting practice at a pace his nervous system liked.

He replaced adrenaline with intention, chaos with clarity, urgency with steadiness.

He didn't get smaller — he got honest.

And honesty gave him back his power.

The Second-Act Filter: Choose by Capacity, Not Expectation

Capacity is the new currency of midlife.

Choosing by capacity means asking:

- What can I sustain without self-betrayal?
- What pace protects my health?
- What boundaries create peace?
- What drains me even if it's "free"?
- What nourishes me even if it takes effort?
- Where have I been pretending I have more capacity than I do?
- Where have I underestimated my capacity because of old fear?

Choosing by expectation recreates your past.

Choosing by capacity creates your future.

The Three Agreements

Agreement 1: I will not punish myself for the years I spent surviving.

Agreement 2: I will not rush myself into a life that doesn't fit.

Agreement 3: I will honour who I'm becoming more than who I once had to be.

KEY TAKEAWAYS

- Identity shapes behaviour more than intention.
- Act Two begins with inner permission, not external validation.
- You are no longer performing — you are choosing.
- Alignment creates more momentum than pressure ever has.
- A self-designed life is a financial strategy, not a luxury.

Reflection Prompts

Take these slowly — this isn't homework. It's inquiry.

- Who am I becoming now?
- What matters to me in this chapter?
- What am I no longer willing to sacrifice?
- What dreams are resurfacing?
- What does freedom feel like now?
- What pace is kind to my body?
- What would future-me thank me for?

Finish:

Act Two isn't about more — it's about mine.

Tiny Steps to Begin

Choose one. Only one.

□ Schedule a monthly "vision hour" (tea, warmth, notebook).

□ Add one joy to your week.

□ Release one draining expectation.

□ Adjust one routine to honour your energy.

□ Practise: "This doesn't work for me anymore."

□ Choose rest one evening without guilt.

□ Set one financial boundary.

□ Remove one pressure you carry only to prove you're capable.

Tiny steps create big freedom.

Act Two doesn't require bravery — it requires alignment.

Your second act isn't recovery.

It isn't compensation for the past.

It is reclamation.

A life designed from the inside out — not from expectation, pressure, or old survival patterns.

From here, we move into the final arc of the book: how to live inside your Slow Money Blueprint with steadiness, simplicity, and self-trust.

Where identity meets action.

Where clarity becomes systems.

Where your life finally feels like your life.

You're not late.

You're right on time — for yourself.

PAUSE HERE.

Drop your shoulders.

Nothing in this chapter is urgent.

Come back into your body before we continue.

"ALIGNMENT OVER ACHIEVEMENT."

CHAPTER 17
THE PROSPER PLAN FOR YOUR MIDLIFE RESET
YOUR SLOW, STEADY, NERVOUS-SYSTEM-FRIENDLY BLUEPRINT FOR ACT TWO.

The Prosper Plan Begins With Steadiness, Not Speed

For decades, the world taught you that financial progress required force — hustle, urgency, pressure, speed.

Start now. Push harder. Don't stop.

But midlife brings its own truth: intensity doesn't last.

It burns. It fractures. It drains — pulling you into short-term survival instead of long-term stability.

Steadiness, however — the kind born from clarity, calm pacing, and nervous-system alignment — lasts.

In your 20s, you built identity.

In your 30s, you built responsibility.

In your 40s, 50s, and beyond, you build capacity.

The Prosper Plan is designed for this exact season.

Not to turn you into a high-performance machine — but to support you as a well-resourced, well-paced human being.

This is not a program you "complete."

It's a rhythm you live inside.

Why Midlife Needs a Different Plan

Midlife isn't the beginning — it's the middle of a story already shaped by emotional labour, caregiving, health shifts, quiet grief, financial responsibilities, invisible workloads, hormonal changes, career pivots, and seasons of survival.

Traditional finance assumes unlimited energy, linear progress, and a perfectly regulated nervous system — a fantasy that doesn't match real midlife lives.

This season doesn't need rigid frameworks.

It needs gentle scaffolding that honours your bandwidth, your wisdom, and your lived reality.

The Prosper Plan meets you exactly where you are — not where anyone tells you you "should be."

The Prosper Plan™ is your personal midlife wealth blueprint. It pulls everything in this book into one place: your safety base, your debt approach, your everyday money system, your investing choices, your work and energy, and your future security.

It isn't a rigid schedule.

It's a living plan that flexes with your life — while still moving you in the same direction: **steady, grounded wealth**.

Reset, Not Reinvention

Hold this truth gently:

You are not starting again.

You are resetting from a place of wisdom.

Everything you've lived — the detours, the setbacks, the wins, the losses, the survival seasons — is now your advantage.

You're not a beginner.

You're a seasoned, self-aware human with boundaries, clarity, and emotional intelligence.

Why We Start With Nervous-System Wealth

Money decisions don't come from your spreadsheet — they come from your body.

A regulated nervous system:

- thinks clearly
- spends intentionally
- stays consistent
- resists panic
- makes wiser choices
- maintains momentum

A distressed nervous system:

- avoids logins
- overspends to self-soothe
- forgets plans
- panics at headlines
- collapses into all-or-nothing
- makes reactive decisions you later regret

So the Prosper Plan begins with:

Calm first.

Choices second.

Consistency third.

Traditional finance says: "Push harder."

Slow Money says: "Regulate first. Then decide."

Because when your body is calm, your future becomes possible again.

Your Midlife Advantage

You have something younger adults don't:

- discernment
- clarity
- boundaries
- pattern recognition
- emotional intelligence
- self-awareness
- a deeper understanding of what matters
- a refusal to waste time on what doesn't

Midlife investors don't succeed because they move fast.

They succeed because they move correctly.

You're no longer chasing noise.

You're choosing alignment.

You're protecting your peace.

That is wealth.

The Prosper Plan Is a Companion, Not a Challenge

This isn't a 90-day sprint.

It isn't an achievement system.

It isn't a pressure cooker.

It's a companion that:

- lowers stress
- increases clarity
- builds momentum
- honours your energy
- simplifies everything
- removes shame
- restores nervous-system safety

It works even when you're: tired, caregiving, overwhelmed, rebuilding, short on time, in a setback, or feeling "behind."

Because you do not need perfection.

You need a plan that supports the human you are now.

THE FOUR PILLARS

1 Stabilise

Create calm and clarity. Build emotional safety and reclaim your financial ground.

2 Systemise

Make good decisions automatic. Remove reliance on motivation.

3 Grow Gently

Increase slowly, sustainably, wisely. Choose opportunities that support your life — not drain it.

4 Protect the Future

Ensure long-term dignity, safety, choices, and emotional peace.

This isn't about being "sorted."

It's about being supported.

A Grounding Pause

Hand on heart. Breathe in once, slowly. Soften your shoulders.

Say quietly:

"I build wealth at the pace of my nervous system."

"I am not late. I am arriving now."

"This time, I do it with clarity and calm."

Good. Your second act begins here — with presence, not pressure.

PILLAR ONE — STABILISE

Your nervous-system-first foundation

Most financial plans start with numbers.

The Prosper Plan starts with capacity.

In midlife, the issue is rarely knowledge.

It's bandwidth.

Stabilisation is your reset point — not something you "graduate" from, but something you return to whenever life gets loud.

Stability looks like:

- waking without dread
- logging in without bracing
- having one clear place your money flows
- feeling steady enough to make decisions
- not spiralling when surprises appear

Stabilisation isn't lack of ambition.

It's the soil ambition grows from.

The Five Anchors of Stabilisation

Anchor 1 — Financial Visibility Without Panic

Your new rule: *"I look once a week — gently, without judgement."*

Anchor 2 — The Essential Spending Snapshot

Not a spreadsheet. A snapshot:

1 What must be paid monthly?

2 What is essential for stability?

3 What supports wellbeing?

4 What drains you financially or emotionally?

Anchor 3 — Automated Safety Nets

Automation removes guilt, decision fatigue, inconsistency, and avoidance.

Start with: direct debits, minimum payments, tiny weekly saving, a "Future Me" pot.

Anchor 4 — Emotional Decluttering

Ask: *"What one thing would make this feel 10% calmer?"*

Do that. One knot at a time.

Anchor 5 — Your First Buffer (Tiny Emergency Fund)

You don't need three months right now.

You need evidence. Even £50–£200 changes the nervous system.

Evidence → calm → clarity → momentum.

THE STABILISE RESET

Your Four-Week Foundation (Built for Real Midlife Lives)

This is the part you return to any time life shakes you.

Not punishment. Not restriction. Not "starting over."

Stabilisation is the adult version of safety.

Week 1 — Look + Label (Without Panic)

Goal: **Visibility without shame.**

Do this:

□ Choose ONE "money home" (a notebook, Notes app, or a single document).

□ List your essentials: mortgage/rent, utilities, food, transport, phone.

□ Log into your main bank account once. Just observe.

□ Write one calming line: *"I'm looking at reality, not judging myself."*

Tiny action (pick one):

□ Open accounts for 30 seconds.

□ Pay one bill you've avoided.

□ Delete one stressful finance email thread.

Week 2 — Stabilise the Floor

Goal: **Essentials covered. Chaos reduced.**

Do this:

□ Set up/confirm direct debits for essentials.

□ Cancel or pause ONE non-essential drain (even temporary).
□ Make an "Essentials Only" plan for the next 7 days.
□ Create one micro-rule: *"No shame spending, no panic spending."*
Tiny action (pick one):
□ Move one subscription to "review later."
□ Cook one simple meal at home.
□ Create a small "surprise bills" category (even £5/week).

Week 3 — Build Your First Buffer

Goal: **Evidence of safety.**
Do this:
□ Create a "Future Me" pot (separate savings pot if possible).
□ Set an automatic transfer: £5 / £10 / £25 weekly.
□ Choose your first buffer target: **£100** (or your own number).
□ Celebrate consistency, not amount.
Tiny action (pick one):
□ Sell one unused item.
□ Transfer £1–£5 today.
□ Put a "no spend" boundary on one category for 48 hours.

Week 4 — Soften the Edges

Goal: **Reduce friction + choose one next step.**
Do this:
□ Write a "Money Map Lite": accounts, debts, pensions, key logins.
□ Choose ONE debt focus (no overhauls): *"I'm softening, not fixing."*
□ Pick one weekly ritual time (10 minutes).
□ End with: *"I'm stable enough to build from here."*
Tiny action (pick one):
□ Set a calendar reminder for your weekly check-in.
□ Make one phone call you've delayed.
□ Pick one number to improve by 1% next month.

You've stabilised when:

- you know what must be paid
- you can log in without spiralling

• you have a tiny buffer growing
• you have a weekly rhythm

That's the foundation. That's success.

PILLAR TWO — SYSTEMISE

Your nervous-system-safe structure for predictable progress

Systemising means designing your money life so consistency doesn't depend on energy, motivation, or willpower.

It becomes the path of least resistance.

The Six Systems of Slow Money

System 1 — One Weekly Money Date (10 minutes)

Check balances. Confirm automations. One tiny transfer. Done.

System 2 — Bills Run on Rails

Essentials on direct debit. Minimum debt payments automatic. Late fees eliminated.

System 3 — The "Future Me" Split

A small automatic savings transfer that happens whether you feel motivated or not.

System 4 — Sinking Funds (Real-Life Categories)

Birthdays. Car. Christmas. School costs. Home repairs. Health.

Small monthly amounts prevent financial shocks.

System 5 — The Decision Filter

Before spending: *"Does this support my peace?"*

(If it's a no, it's not guilt — it's information.)

System 6 — The Seasonal Review (Not Obsessive Monitoring)

Quarterly: pensions/investing glance, subscriptions, priorities, and one adjustment.

Systemising is not doing more.

It's doing less — and letting those fewer actions carry you further.

PILLAR THREE — GROW GENTLY

Growth that honours your season, not your stress

Midlife growth isn't loud. It isn't frantic. It isn't fuelled by adrenaline.

Growth in this season is **discerned, not chased**. Aligned, not rushed. Intentional, not performative.

Gentle growth doesn't mean small growth.

It means **sustainable growth** — the kind that doesn't collapse when life gets busy, your energy dips, or your nervous system gets loud.

Midlife teaches you:

- rushing leads to redoing
- forcing leads to freezing
- overcommitting leads to collapsing
- acting from fear creates regret

So we grow like adults now: **slow enough to stay intact, steady enough to compound.**

The Five Principles of Gentle Growth

1) Improve by 1%, not 100%

Your nervous system can handle 1%. And 1% compounds.

Examples:

- increase pension contributions by 1%
- add £10 to investing
- raise your emergency fund transfer by £5
- reduce one recurring cost
- strengthen one boundary that protects capacity

Small is sustainable. Sustainable becomes inevitable.

2) Choose opportunities — don't chase them

Chasing belongs to Act One. Choosing belongs to Act Two.

Run every "opportunity" through three questions:

- Does this honour my energy?
- Does this support long-term safety?
- Does this feel peaceful or pressured?

If it costs your nervous system, it isn't wealth.

3) Let money work while you rest

Midlife is the season of:
✔ automation
✔ simple investing
✔ low fees
✔ consistent contributions
✔ boring brilliance
Your systems carry the progress — not your willpower.

4) Build abundance through capacity, not overwork

Capacity is currency: sleep, clarity, regulation, boundaries, focus.

When you have more inner room, you make better decisions without force.

5) Celebrate sustainability, not speed

Speed looks impressive. Sustainability changes lives.

Your new mantra: **Stable is successful.**

The Three Paths of Gentle Growth

Path 1 — Strengthen what already exists

Often the highest ROI work is unglamorous:

- renegotiate bills
- patch financial leaks
- increase contributions slightly
- refine budgets into snapshots
- strengthen boundaries

Tiny edits, major long-term impact.

Path 2 — Gentle income expansion (capacity-aligned)

Not hustle. Not exhaustion. Just one sustainable lever.

Examples:

- one consulting client
- one monthly service
- one small digital product

• seasonal part-time work
• fractional/advisory roles

One calm extra stream can change everything — because it lasts.

Path 3 — Grow through subtraction

Sometimes wealth comes from removing what drains you:

• chaotic schedules
• avoidable fees
• perfectionism
• emotional over-functioning
• commitments that cost too much energy

Subtraction increases bandwidth. Bandwidth increases wealth.

The Gentle Growth Ladder™

You climb at the pace your life can hold.

1 Stabilise
2 Automate
3 Increase by 1%
4 Add one gentle income lever (optional)
5 Simplify + subtract
6 Strengthen boundaries
7 Review seasonally

No rushing. No shame. Just forward movement.

Tiny Actions (Grow Gently Edition)

Pick one this month:

□ Increase one automation by £5
□ Cancel one "leak" (subscription/fee)
□ Put 1% more into pension/retirement account
□ Add one small "Future Me" transfer
□ Create a 30-minute weekly capacity block (to protect your energy)

PILLAR FOUR — PROTECT THE FUTURE

Long-term dignity is a form of wealth

In your earlier years, the future felt theoretical.

In midlife, the future becomes real: a real body, a real home, real choices, real vulnerabilities — and real freedom.

Protection isn't pessimism.

Protection is **care stretched across time.**

The Six Protection Areas of the Prosper Plan

1) Legal peace papers

This is not fear. This is future kindness.

Your "Peace Papers" include:

- will
- power of attorney / lasting power of attorney
- healthcare directive / advance decision (where relevant)
- updated beneficiaries
- key documents + passwords
- someone who knows where everything is

2) Housing stability (options, not pressure)

You're not deciding today. You're creating choices.

Questions to explore gently:

- Do I stay, downsize, or relocate someday?
- What environment supports my future body?
- What home costs might rise?
- What sinking fund protects repairs/maintenance?

Options are emotional wealth.

3) Income continuity + "protect the asset" thinking

The asset isn't your pension. It's you.

Protection includes:

- sustainable workload
- boundaries
- annual health checks
- recovery rhythms
- emergency buffer

• considering income protection insurance (where appropriate)

4) Retirement / Act Three structure (simple beats perfect)

You don't need a flawless plan. You need a maintainable one:

• steady contributions
• low fees
• simple investments
• occasional reviews
• reducing high-interest debt
• a "Future Me Fund"

5) Emotional and social support networks

Financial isolation is a hidden risk.

Protection includes:

• friendships
• community ties
• people who know your real life
• routines that keep you connected

Money matters — but connection shapes older years more than most people expect.

6) Boundaries that guard future peace

In midlife, boundaries become financial tools:

• "I can help, but I can't rescue."
• "Not this month."
• "My pace matters."
• "I prioritise my own future."

Boundaries protect your money, your time, your energy — and your dignity.

The Protection Checklist (Calm Version)

Choose one category per month. No overwhelm.

□ Legal: update will/beneficiaries OR book appointment

□ Admin: create an "Emergency Folder" (digital or physical)
□ Housing: start a home sinking fund (even £10/week)
□ Health: book one overdue appointment
□ Support: identify your "safe people" list
□ Systems: share where key info lives (one trusted person)

Tiny Action (Protect the Future Edition)

□ Ask yourself: *If I was suddenly unavailable, who needs to find what?*

Then take one step: write one password location, one contact, one document folder.

Bringing All Four Pillars Together

Stabilise: I create safety before strategy.

Systemise: I make good things automatic.

Grow Gently: I increase at a pace that supports me.

Protect the Future: I honour the person I'm becoming.

And your Prosper Plan compass stays the same:

"I build wealth at the pace of my nervous system."

KEY TAKEAWAYS

- Your second act is not a downgrade — it's an upgrade built on truth.
- You're building a life that matches your real values, not old expectations.
- The next chapter prioritises energy, alignment, and agency.
- You don't need a reinvention — just a clear path and calm steps.
- Midlife gives you the wisdom to design intentionally, not reactively.

Tiny Action

□ Ask yourself: Who needs access to your financial logins or plans if you were suddenly unavailable? Then take one small step toward sharing it.

Reflection Prompts — Your Prosper Identity

- Who am I becoming?
- What already feels calmer?
- Where have I stabilised without noticing?
- What identity shift wants support next?
- What does my Slow Money life look like six months ahead?

Finish:
"I choose a life built on clarity, steadiness, and self-trust."

. You now have the foundation.

Next, we turn it into a **six-month living rhythm** —

the structure that makes the Prosper Plan real, gentle, and sustainable.

Chapter 18 gives you the roadmap:

- month-by-month
- paced for real midlife lives
- anchored in energy, capacity, and clarity
- built for relief, not pressure

A soft, steady season of rebuilding.

You're not starting over— you're starting supported.

“GENTLE DOES NOT MEAN WEAK.”

THE SIX-MONTH SLOW MONEY RESET AT A GLANCE

MONTH 1 — GROUNDING

- Gentle clarity
- Spending awareness
- Emotional bandwidth check
- One tiny step a week

MONTH 2 — CLARITY

- Numbers written down
- Debts listed
- Safety baseline set
- First Snowball Plus™ payment

MONTH 3 — SAFETY

- Emergency buffer (even £10–£20 counts)
- Nervous-system financial cues
- Money boundaries introduced

MONTH 4 — STRATEGY

- Pension review
- Savings structure
- Income tweaks
- Subscription audit

MONTH 5 — MOMENTUM

- Automation
- Rituals
- Refined spending patterns
- Identity strengthening

MONTH 6 — INTEGRATION

- Long-term habits
- Seasonal reviews
- Soft planning
- Second adulthood alignment

Slow Money is not a race —

CHAPTER 18

THE SIX-MONTH SLOW MONEY RESET™

A DIFFERENT KIND OF RESET — ONE THAT RESPECTS YOUR SEASON

Midlife change doesn't shout.

It doesn't demand a montage or a transformation arc.

Real midlife reset energy is quieter — and infinitely deeper.

It feels like:

- breathing again after years of bracing
- doing less, but doing it consistently
- choosing rhythm over adrenaline
- accepting "good enough" instead of chasing perfect
- letting the nervous system lead, not fear
- remembering how to trust yourself gently

This Reset isn't a challenge.

It's a companion — a handrail for the textured months when motivation dips, pressure rises, or life asks more of you than you expected.

You don't push yourself through this plan.

You arrive in it — with honesty, with softness, with the energy you have today.

This is the Slow Money way:

steady, sustainable, self-respecting growth.

This isn't a program — it's a seasonal rhythm.

Six months is long enough to create identity-level change, and gentle enough to avoid overwhelm.

Before we dive in, a small reminder: this six-month reset is a framework to support you — not a promise of a specific result. Some months will feel spacious, others will feel textured or demanding — that's part of real life, not a sign that you're off track. Progress in midlife is rarely linear, but it is absolutely possible when you move steadily and stay kind to yourself.

How the Reset Works

Each month gives you:

✔ **One theme**
✔ **One emotional goal**
✔ **One practical money goal**
✔ **One anchoring habit**
✔ **One tiny celebration ritual**
✔ **A weekly check-in (5–10 minutes)**

No speed.
No shame.
No pressure.
Just six months of gentle, compounding steadiness.
This isn't about fast success.
It's about stability that lasts a lifetime.

MONTH ONE — The Grounding Month

Theme: Stabilise & Breathe
Emotional Goal: Safety
Money Goal: Visibility + Clarity

You cannot build a future from panic.
You build it from truth-telling and nervous-system softening.

Many people arrive here exhausted. Exhaustion isn't failure — it's the receipt of everything you carried:

- financially
- emotionally
- hormonally
- energetically
- mentally

So we begin with grounding, not strategy.

Your Month One Focus

- Gather a soft overview of your accounts (no sorting, no judging)
- One weekly money check-in (5–10 minutes only)
- Begin your tiny emergency buffer
- Create a soothing ritual for money days
- Unfollow fear-based financial noise
- Remove shame from every financial conversation

Your grounding sentence:

"I can face my life without flinching."

This is emotional wealth — the kind that makes everything else possible.

Tiny Actions — Choose One

□ Save £5/$5 weekly
□ Organise direct debits
□ Rename one pot "Future Me"
□ Light a candle before looking at numbers
□ Open your money app once without doing anything

Celebration Ritual

Write down one thing you survived.

One season that required strength you didn't know you had.

That resilience is the first deposit into your future.

Next month, we'll gently bring in clarity — not pressure — so you can see what's true without overwhelm.

MONTH TWO — The Foundation Month

Theme: Systems Over Willpower

Emotional Goal: Calm Control

Money Goal: Automate the Basics

This is the month everything begins to feel different —
not because the numbers change quickly,
but because **the heavy lifting moves from your mind to your systems**.

Motivation becomes optional.
Reliability becomes built in.

Your Month Two Focus

✔ **1. Automate all essential bills**
✔ **2. Automate minimum debt payments**
✔ **3. Start one micro-investment (£10–£25)**
✔ **4. Spend-tracking: once weekly only**
✔ **5. Establish one energy boundary**

Your finances follow your energy.
Protect your energy → protect your money.

Why Systems Beat Motivation

Motivation is chaotic.
Systems are calming, adult, and dependable.
Systems don't spiral.
Systems don't judge you.
Systems don't burn out.
They protect your future when life gets busy.
This month, they begin protecting you too.

This Month's Mantra

"My systems protect me when life gets busy."

Tiny Actions — Choose One

□ Automate one micro-deposit
□ Unfollow three draining accounts
□ Practice: "Let me think about it."
□ Set calendar reminders for payments

□ Add a snack + water to your desk (prevents impulsive spending)

Celebration Ritual

A low-cost comfort:

- bath
- walk
- early night
- favourite film
- fresh sheets
- quiet hour alone

Celebrate the shift from pressure → support.

Automation is self-respect.

Next month, we'll add simple structure at your pace, turning clarity into calm, doable steps.

MONTH THREE — The Strength Month

Theme: Build Stability Without Force

Emotional Goal: Confidence

Money Goal: Debt + Savings Rhythm

Confidence returns here —
not because everything is fixed,
but because you're moving from fear → agency.
Your systems work.
Your foundation is steadier.
Your nervous system feels safer.
Now we strengthen, gently.

Your Month Three Focus

✔ 1. Choose your debt method

A. **Snowball** — smallest balance first

B. **Avalanche** — highest interest first

C. **Snowball Plus** — *your* hybrid method

- emotional wins first

• mathematical efficiency next
• nervous-system safety always

This is not punishment.

This is predictability.

Snowball Plus works best in midlife because it balances emotion, mathematics, and nervous-system safety.

✔ 2. Create ONE sinking fund

Just one.

A single buffer prevents future panic.

✔ 3. Observe spending patterns with curiosity

Not criticism.

Not shame.

Just data.

✔ 4. Add one nervous-system reset for money stress

Tea before decisions.

Breathing.

Walks.

Body scans.

Regulated brains make better financial choices.

This Month's Script

"I reduce debt in ways that protect my peace."

Tiny Actions — Choose One

□ Start a Joy Fund
□ Label your sinking fund
□ Schedule a "Financial Reset Walk"
□ Write one kind sentence to yourself
□ Declutter one financial stressor

Celebration Ritual

Choose softness:

• blanket + tea
• a quiet hour with a book
• a bath
• gentle playlist

Celebrate the fact you're showing up differently now.

That alone changes everything.

Next month, we shift from income alignment to future dignity — one of the most empowering phases of the reset.

MONTH FOUR — The Alignment Month

Theme: Earn With Integrity

Emotional Goal: Self-Respect

Money Goal: Energy-Aligned Income

This month unites your financial life with your identity.

Not through reinvention.

Through alignment.

You shift from:

• performing → honouring

• proving → pacing

• obligation → autonomy

This is earning with dignity.

Your Month Four Focus

✔ 1. Perform an Energy Audit at Work

Ask:

• What drains me?

• What energises me?

• What work feels meaningful?

• Where do I over-give?

✔ 2. Set ONE work boundary

Small boundaries change entire income trajectories.

✔ 3. Explore "Curiosity Income"

Not hustle.

Not pressure.

Just possibility.

This is not a side-hustle month — it's a self-respect month.

✔ 4. Build a Competence File

A folder, note, or document of:

• compliments

• achievements

• forgotten strengths
• proof of your natural value

Midlife brilliance often goes unremembered.

This restores accuracy.

This Month's Script

"I work like someone who respects their energy."

Tiny Actions — Choose One

□ One hour weekly of curiosity income
□ Set one work boundary
□ List your effortless strengths
□ Ask for support in one area
□ Delete one draining expectation

Celebration Ritual

Honour your worth:

• slow breakfast
• flowers
• early finish
• quiet walk
• journaling

You're shifting from survival → self-respect.

Next month, we'll build on your progress with small, sustainable upgrades that feel supportive, not demanding.

MONTH FIVE — The Dignity Month

Theme: Future Me Deserves Ease

Emotional Goal: Agency

Money Goal: Long-Term Protection

This is your future-protection month —
not fear-based, not crisis-based.
Dignity-based.

You're not planning for disaster.

You're planning for comfort, clarity, and choice.

Your Month Five Focus

✔ **1. Update beneficiaries**

Five minutes.

Huge peace.

✔ **2. Review Will + Power of Attorney**

It doesn't have to be perfect.

It just needs to exist.

✔ **3. Explore housing and ageing preferences**

Not decisions — options.

✔ **4. Make a Later-Life Joy List**

This list will matter more than any pension calculation.

It doesn't need to be perfect — it just needs to exist.

This Month's Script

"Planning ahead is an act of self-love."

Tiny Actions — Choose One

□ Create a "Future Me" folder

□ Write three comforts you want in later life

□ Update one beneficiary

□ Draft a paragraph: "Life at 70 feels like…"

□ Share your wishes with someone you trust

Celebration Ritual

Choose a gesture that honours the older you:

- nourishing meal
- vitamins
- a walk
- early night
- journaling
- self-care appointment

Dignity is wealth.

Next month, we'll weave everything together, creating a money life that feels steady, sovereign, and truly yours.

MONTH SIX — The Becoming Month

Theme: Embodiment

Emotional Goal: Identity Shift

Money Goal: Integration & Strengthening Systems

Month Six is where everything integrates.

Where action becomes identity.

Where behaviour becomes belief.

Where wealth becomes rhythm.

You aren't "improving" anymore.

You're **living** differently.

This is embodiment.

You're no longer practicing Slow Money — you're embodying it in the small, steady decisions that build long-term dignity.

Your Month Six Focus

✔ **1. Increase automation (gently)**

£/$5–25

It's not the amount —

it's the identity shift:

"I strengthen my future automatically."

✔ **2. Choose your long-term pace**

Gentle.

Steady.

Solid.

All valid.

Choose the one your nervous system can sustain.

✔ **3. Test ONE earning idea**

Just testing, not leaping.

✔ **4. Review spending for joy alignment**

Curate, don't cut.

✔ **5. Write your Act Two Money Philosophy**

This becomes your compass.

This Month's Script

"I live my wealth, gently."

• • •

Six months didn't reinvent you — they revealed the version of you that was waiting for space.

KEY TAKEAWAYS

• You're not behind — you're right on schedule for a human life.

• Your future doesn't need urgency; it needs leadership, clarity, and care.

• Slow, grounded action always outperforms panic-driven change.

• You now have structure, identity, and rhythm — the foundations of calm wealth.

• The second act begins not with speed, but with self-trust.

Tiny Actions — Choose One

□ Start one aligned habit

□ Schedule quarterly reviews

□ Share your new boundary with someone

□ Begin a "What I Believe About Money Now" document

□ Put a note somewhere visible: "I belong to my future."

Celebration Ritual

A candle.
A walk.
Fresh flowers.
A nourishing meal.
A slow afternoon.
You're celebrating not the plan —
but the person you've become.

From here, your Slow Money rhythm continues — not as a plan to finish, but as a life you're ready to live.

Closing the Reset

You didn't rush.

You didn't collapse.

You didn't force yourself through pressure or panic.

You stabilised.

You softened.

You systemised.

You strengthened.

You aligned.

You honoured your future.

You restored trust with yourself.

You built wealth from your nervous system outward.

You didn't "start over."

You returned to yourself — the part of you that always knew you were capable of more than survival.

This reset doesn't end.

It becomes the quiet architecture beneath the life you're choosing now.

You didn't fall behind— you lived, you adapted, you carried more than anyone saw. Now you rise with steadiness, not urgency.

From here, we move into the closing reflection —

the chapter that ties everything together and escorts the reader gently into their Act Two life:

- steady
- sovereign
- self-trusting
- future-ready
- grounded

You're not ending something — you're beginning a season where your money, your energy, and your identity finally move in the same direction.

"I BUILD QUIETLY, BECAUSE IT LASTS."

PART IV — YOU'RE NOT BEHIND

CHAPTER 19

YOU'RE NOT BEHIND – MOVING FORWARD WITH SLOW, STEADY WEALTH

You Didn't Start Over — You Came Home

You didn't pick up this book to become someone new — you picked it up to return to someone true.

Your life hasn't been linear.

It has been human — beautifully, painfully, courageously human.

A life shaped by:

- detours you never planned
- responsibilities you carried quietly
- seasons of survival
- years of giving more than you had
- decisions made from love, fear, or necessity — or simply doing your best with what you had
- moments where you held everyone else together
- chapters where you forgot your own needs

You didn't fall behind.

You lived — fully, messily, bravely.

And now, in midlife, you finally turn toward yourself with tenderness instead of tension.

This book wasn't a financial overhaul.

It was a self-permission ceremony.

A remembering.

A reclamation.

A reset rooted not in discipline — but in dignity.

You didn't hustle.

You didn't sprint.

You didn't force yourself into change.

You stabilised.

You softened.

You strengthened your systems.

You honoured your energy.

You reclaimed your voice.

You rebuilt trust with yourself.

You protected your future.

You stopped treating money as fear and started treating it as support.

You created real safety in your nervous system — the foundation for every future decision.

What Your Younger Self Would Say

If your younger self could see you now, they wouldn't say:

"You're late."

"You should have more."

"You haven't done enough."

They would say:

"We made it."

"We're finally safe."

"You kept going."

"You became someone who takes care of us."

"And now, for the first time in a long time, you are choosing yourself with clarity, not apology."

"Thank you."

That is the quiet miracle of midlife wealth —
not the money itself,
but the stability, clarity, and self-respect behind it.

You Are Not Done — You're Free

Free to:

- build slowly
- rest without earning it
- spend in alignment
- invest without panic
- protect your peace
- choose work that honours your energy
- plan a future that feels like comfort, not fear
- care for others without abandoning yourself
- start again without shame
- age with dignity, not dread

Midlife is not a decline.

It's a refinement.

A sharpening.

A returning.

You are not late.

You are right on time — for the life that fits you now.

Your Act Two Truth

Your second act is not a performance.

It's not reinvention.

It's not a desperate attempt to impress or catch up.

It is a reclamation of:

- your pace
- your clarity
- your wisdom
- your groundedness
- your capacity
- your identity
- your possibilities
- your emotional safety
- your financial sovereignty

You build wealth now the same way you build self-trust — slowly, consistently, compassionately.

Not through adrenaline.

Through alignment.

Not by rushing.
By returning.
Not by force.
By rhythm.
Act Two is where you become the custodian of your life —
not the performer in it.

The Quiet Promise of Slow Money

Slow Money isn't about deprivation.

It's not about being "good with money," or perfectly disciplined, or always in control.

Slow Money is nervous-system-first wealth.

Slow Money is not a money strategy — it's a self-trust strategy.

Identity-first wealth.

Self-respecting wealth.

It's the kind of financial life that feels like an exhale:

- calm
- sustainable
- protective
- aligned
- dignified
- emotionally regulated

This is wealth with longevity —
wealth you can live inside of.
You are not chasing speed anymore.
You are choosing stability.
And stability compounds.

Every philosophy needs one anchor — one sentence that brings you home every time life gets loud.

Your Final Prosperism

If you forget everything in this book —

which you will, because life is real and you're gloriously human — return to this one truth:

"I don't need to be fast.
I just need to be steady — and steady is enough."

Steady builds safety.
Steady builds security.
Steady builds self-trust.
Steady builds a life worth living.
And you — right now, exactly as you are —
are capable of that steadiness.
It's already in you.
You've been practising it your whole life.
This isn't the end.

This is your beginning — a return to clarity, calm, and the version of you who trusts your own timing.

You are ready for your second act — and, more importantly, it's ready to meet you exactly where you are.

SLOW MONEY FRAMEWORKS AT A GLANCE

Calm Money Method™ – Your nervous-system-aware way of running day-to-day money.

Snowball Plus™ – A hybrid debt method combining snowball (emotion) + avalanche (interest rates).

Financial Floor of Safety – The base level of security that lets you breathe.

Prosper Plan™ – Your integrated blueprint for safety, investing, work, and future security.

Slow Money Identity – The version of you who stewards money from calm self-respect, not panic or shame.

THE MIDLIFE SLOW MONEY RESET™ CHECKLISTS

This reset is not a challenge.

It is a *return to steadiness* — one month at a time, one breath at a time, one tiny believable step at a time.

You're not fixing your life — you're befriending it again.

MONTH ONE — THE GROUNDING MONTH

Theme: Stabilise & Breathe

Intent: Awareness without fear

Midlife financial peace doesn't begin with action — it begins with visibility that doesn't activate your flight response.

This month is about facing your life gently, without forcing anything, fixing anything, or judging anything.

Focus

- Weekly money check-in (5–10 mins, soft posture)
- List all accounts + balances (clarity, not critique)
- Begin the first tiny emergency savings habit (£5/$5 is enough)
- Create a soothing ritual for "money moments" — tea, candle, soft playlist, quiet corner
- Reduce financial fear-noise (unfollow panic-based influencers, turn off alerts)

Emotional Cues

• "I can look at my life without flinching."

• Notice: shoulders soften, breath slows, chest loosens, jaw unhooks.

• You're creating *tolerance*, not perfection.

Actions

□ List all accounts + balances (rough is fine)

□ Set weekly check-in time in calendar

□ Save £5/$5 weekly into a "Future Me" pot

□ Create your money ritual (tea, candle, playlist, warm socks — anything regulating)

□ Remove one stress source (alerts, shame triggers, unopened bills pile)

One Win to Celebrate

I showed up for myself.

This alone is a reset.

MONTH TWO — THE FOUNDATION MONTH

Theme: Systems Over Willpower

Intent: Let life support you

Motivation is inconsistent. Systems are loyal.

This month, you build the mechanical backbone that protects you even when life gets messy, busy, hormonal, emotional, or overwhelming.

Focus

• Automate bills + debt minimums

• Set up automatic investing (any sustainable amount)

• Weekly spending check-in (neutral tone)

• Choose one energy boundary to protect yourself

Emotional Cue

• "My systems protect me when life gets busy."

Actions

□ Automate essential payments

□ Set small automatic deposit (£10–£50)

□ Weekly spending review (no shame allowed)

□ Add one boundary (time, work, social, emotional)

□ Review subscriptions once and cancel one

One Win to Celebrate

My life is easier because of choices I made.

MONTH THREE — THE STRENGTH MONTH

Theme: Gentle Momentum

Intent: Reduce stress, not joy

Strength isn't force.

Strength is steadiness — a sense that small, repeated actions are finally holding you rather than draining you.

Focus

- Choose your debt strategy: **Snowball / Avalanche / Snowball Plus**
- Create one sinking fund (car, home, health, joy, repairs)
- Track spending patterns with curiosity (not control)
- Add one emotional regulation tool for financial stress days

Emotional Cue

- "I reduce debt in a way that protects my peace."

Actions

□ Choose your debt method
□ Open one sinking fund (even £5/$5 to start)
□ Weekly emotional spending check-in
□ Add your reset practice (walk, breathwork, journaling, stretch)
□ Speak one kind sentence to yourself daily about money

One Win to Celebrate

I am building steady strength.

Strength, in midlife, is the ability to continue gently.

MONTH FOUR — THE ALIGNMENT MONTH

Theme: Earn With Integrity

Intent: Honour energy, not ego

Midlife income isn't about hustling — it's about working in a way that respects your body, your nervous system, and your second-act identity.

Focus

- Energy audit at work
- One career boundary update
- Explore side-earning curiosity (no pressure)
- Build "Competence File" (what you're brilliant at)

Emotional Cue

- "I earn in a way that honours my life."

Actions

□ Conduct a work energy audit

□ Ask for one support or flexibility adjustment.

□ Spend 1 hour/week exploring gentle earning ideas

□ Start competence file ("things I do well without effort")

□ Release one outdated work identity or expectation

One Win to Celebrate

My work fits me more today than it did last month.

MONTH FIVE — THE DIGNITY MONTH

Theme: Future-Self Respect

Intent: Plan for peace, not fear

Dignity is the quietest form of wealth.

Long-term planning is not morbid — it is midlife maturity.

It is self-love extended across time, ensuring that older-you feels safe, supported, and held.

Focus

- Update beneficiaries
- Review Will / Power of Attorney
- Map housing + ageing preferences
- Create Later-Life Joy List

Emotional Cue

- "Future me deserves ease."

Actions

□ Review beneficiaries

□ Store will/POA documents safely

□ Note preferences for housing + support

□ Create later-life joy list

□ Share one preference with someone trusted

One Win to Celebrate

Future-me feels supported by present-me.

Note: *Store all documents securely and never share sensitive information electronically unless the platform is verified and encrypted.*

MONTH SIX — THE BECOMING MONTH

Theme: Identity Upgrade

Intent: Live what you've built

This month, the reset stops being something you do — and becomes something you are.

Focus

- Increase auto-deposits slightly
- Review spending alignment
- Softly test one earning idea
- Schedule quarterly money check-ins
- Declare your Act Two Money Philosophy

Emotional Cue

- "I am someone who tends to my life with respect."

Actions

□ Increase automatic deposit by £5–£25
□ Review: Does my spending match my values?
□ Try one tiny earning step
□ Schedule quarterly check-ins
□ Write your money philosophy (1–3 sentences)

One Win to Celebrate

I live differently now. It shows.

END-OF-RESET REFLECTION PAGE

Answer slowly. No rushing.

How has my relationship with money changed?
How has my self-talk softened?
What feels easier now?
Where am I gentler with myself?
What pace supports me now?
What identity am I stepping into?
Where do I feel more sovereign than I did six months ago?
Final Line to Write:

I don't chase wealth — I grow it slowly, because I'm building a life I can live inside.

YOUR FINAL REFLECTION

Take a quiet moment.

Breathe once, slowly.

Ask yourself:

- What feels different in me now?
- What has softened?
- What have I stabilised without even noticing?
- Where do I feel more capable, more grounded, more aware?
- What part of my financial life feels possible again?
- What one gentle step am I ready to take next?

Write one sentence to carry forward:

"My wealth grows at the pace of my nervous system."

And one promise to yourself:

"I will build my future with steadiness, not stress."

You are ready for Act Two —

ready to live a financial life that feels like an exhale.

RESOURCES & NEXT STEPS

A CURATED GUIDE TO PROTECT YOUR PEACE, STRENGTHEN YOUR FUTURE, AND KEEP YOUR RESET ALIVE

You do not need to explore all of this at once.

Treat these resources like a calm library, not a to-do list.

Pick what applies to your season. You are not catching up — you are continuing, wisely.

Digital Safety Reminder

As more financial tasks move online, always protect your information. Never share one-time codes, passwords, or verification details with anyone – including people claiming to be banks, platforms, or advisers. Use official websites and apps only, double-check web addresses, and be cautious of urgent messages or pressure-based requests. If something feels rushed, confusing, or "too good to be true," pause. Calm decisions are safer decisions.

How to Use This Section

These tools aren't steps — they're supports. Start with one of each:

- One tool for clarity
- One tool for saving/investing
- One form of support
- One gentle learning source

And then stop.

Integration comes from **less, done steadily**, not more, consumed frantically.

Your nervous system needs pacing. Your future needs structure. We do both here.

If you'd like support turning this book into a living plan, you'll find companion tools, trackers, and templates at **slowmoneymovement.com.** Think of them as your practical bridge between what you've just read and what you'll do next — built in the same Slow Money spirit: steady, grounded, and human.

FOUNDATIONS: TOOLS FOR FINANCIAL CALM

These are not tasks — they are supports.

Banking & Saving Platforms (Ease First, Always)

🇬🇧 **UK**

- **Chase UK** — simple savings, round-ups, effortless app
- **Nationwide** — reliable savings with member-owned stability
- **Monzo** — "pots" for budgeting, instant transfers, clear visibility
- **Starling Bank** — strong budgeting tools, excellent for personal and business use

🇺🇸 **US**

- **Ally Bank** — high-yield savings with strong automation
- **Capital One 360** — no-fee accounts and easy automatic transfers
- **SoFi** — modern savings + investing in one place
- **Fidelity / Vanguard** — trusted long-term options with low fees

Choose the bank that makes habits easier, not the one that looks impressive.

Investing Platforms (Calm, Long-Term, Proven)

🇬🇧 **UK**

- **Vanguard UK** — low-cost index funds, simple to maintain
- **AJ Bell / Interactive Investor** — strong for pensions and ISAs
- **Moneybox** — tiny-steps investing with round-ups

🇺🇸 **US**

- **Vanguard** — the gold standard for slow, steady index investing

• **Fidelity / Charles Schwab** — excellent support + broad index fund options

• **Betterment** — a gentle, automated investing route

The goal isn't to pick "the best."

The goal is to choose the one you'll use *consistently*.

Pension & Retirement Guidance (Peace Through Clarity)

🇬🇧 **UK**

• **MoneyHelper.gov.uk** — clear, unbiased pension explanations

• **Gov.uk State Pension Forecast** — check your current entitlement

• **Pension Wise** — free, expert midlife-retirement guidance

• **National Insurance Credit Info** — understand and fill NI gaps

• **The Money and Pensions Service** — central hub for pensions, budgeting, and debt support

🇺🇸 **US**

• **SSA.gov** — Social Security estimates and projections

• **Investor.gov** — trustworthy investing and retirement education

• **401(k) + IRA Catch-Up Guides** — understand allowances and contribution boosts

Checking your pension is not a judgement — it's self-respect.

You can learn at 50 exactly as successfully as at 30, often with more wisdom and a calmer sense of urgency.

Debt & Protection Tools

• **Snowball Plus method** — (as shared in book)

• **Annual credit report** (UK & US free services)

• **Insurance review** (life, income protection, home)

• **Will & Power of Attorney**

This is not gloomy preparation.

It's **adult dignity**.

Future-you will breathe easier because of this work.

Protection isn't pessimistic — it's compassionate.

Remember: retirement ages, State Pension rules, Social Security benefits, tax bands, and allowances change over time and differ by country. Always check the latest guidance for your region before making decisions based on any example in this book.

Gentle Support & Advice

You do not have to figure this out alone.

Professional Help

- **Financial Planner / Adviser** – interview, don't surrender control
- **Debt charity or advisor** (UK: StepChange, US: NFCC)
- **Therapist familiar with money anxiety**
- **Career / midlife transitions coach** (optional, not urgent)

Peer Support

- Quiet money communities
- Slow wealth groups
- Midlife support circles
- Trusted friend with similar values

Choose financial company that **reduces adrenaline, not raises it**.

How to Talk to a Financial Adviser

Use these questions:

- *"How do you get paid?"*
- *"Do you recommend products you earn from?"*
- *"Can we go slowly — I learn best step by step?"*
- *"I care about peace and simplicity — can you help me build that?"*
- *"Please explain without jargon."*

If they rush you, shame you, or try to impress you with complexity?

You leave.

Your future is not a performance.

It's a partnership.

Books & Gentle Learning

Midlife reinvention + slow finance:

- *The Psychology of Money* — Morgan Housel
- *Four Thousand Weeks* — Oliver Burkeman
- *The Next Right Thing* — Emily P. Freeman
- *Die With Zero* — Bill Perkins *(philosophy, not prescription)*

You don't need to consume everything.
Pick one.
Read slowly.
This is not school.
This is nourishment.

Mental Health & Crisis Support

If you ever feel overwhelmed or stuck:

🇬🇧 UK

- **NHS mental health support**
- **Samaritans** – talk, no judgement
- **Mind UK**

🇺🇸 US

- **988 Lifeline**
- **NAMI**
- **MentalHealth.gov**

Financial stress can feel like danger.
Your body isn't dramatic — it's protecting you.
Support is strength, not failure.

SLOW MONEY MOVEMENT™ RESOURCES

THE SLOW MONEY STARTER STACK™ (Free Toolkit)

Your starter set of tools designed to create calm, capacity, and clarity — even in the busiest midlife season:

- Family Financial Resilience Checklist
- Solo Financial Resilience Checklist
- Slow Money Allowance Tracker
- Slow Money Mini Debt Tracker
- Crypto Literacy Worksheet
- Global Family Finance Planner
- Beginner-friendly budgeting and planning tools

Access the full free stack at: **slowmoneymovement.com/the-vault**

THE SLOW MONEY STARTER DASHBOARD™ (Paid Upgrade)

A deeper, structured toolkit for readers ready to take the next step, including:

• Fillable Monthly Budget Template
• Automated Net Worth Tracker
• Prosper Path™ One-Page Roadmap
• Weekly Wealth Habits Tracker
• Bonus: Prosperisms™ Quote Cards
• Lifetime updates

Find it at: **slowmoneymovement.com/the-vault**

THE SNOWBALL PLUS™ DEBT PLANNER

Your hybrid Snowball/Avalanche system — designed for calm, sustainable debt momentum rather than pressure and panic.

This planner helps you:

• Organise multiple debts
• Prioritise them in a nervous-system-safe sequence
• Track wins
• Build monthly clarity
• Stay committed without burnout

Available inside the Toolkit or as a standalone tool.

Find it at: **slowmoneymovement.com/the-vault**

FAMILY FINANCE RESOURCES

A curated library for parents and guardians, including:

• Kids & Teens Savings Trackers
• Family Financial Resilience Workbook
• Digital Age Allowance Planner
• Teen Budgeting Worksheets
• Family Investing Guides (ISAs, JISAs, 529s, custodial accounts)
• Future of Family Finance FAQs

Updated regularly at: **slowmoneymovement.com**

THE WEALTH HABITS LIBRARY

Short, practical guides on:

• Slow investing
• Midlife pension calming
• Energy-led earning
• Identity-based money behaviour
• Emotional wealth
• Nervous-system money rhythms

Perfect for dipping in when life feels noisy.

Updated regularly at: **slowmoneymovement.com/blog**

THE SLOW MONEY NEWSLETTER

Weekly calm-wealth prompts, nervous-system-safe planning tips, and practical money clarity for your second act.

No overwhelm. No hustle. Just steady guidance.

Subscribe at: **slowmoneymovement.com**

FOLLOW THE MOVEMENT

For calm-wealth posts, slow investing, midlife money wisdom, and steady financial encouragement:

Instagram / TikTok / Pinterest: @slowmoneymovement

A Final Compass

Keep one truth close:

I build at the pace my nervous system can sustain.

And one sentence for your wallet, mirror, or notes app:

Slow is not late.

Slow is wise.

Slow is wealth.

You have not been behind.

You have been becoming.

Now you continue —

softly, steadily, in your power.

You don't need all of this. You only need the next gentle step.

FURTHER LISTENING & READING

FOR NERVOUS-SYSTEM-FRIENDLY PERSONAL, CAREER, AND MONEY DEVELOPMENT:

You do not need to absorb everything.

Choose one resource, go slowly, and let it land.

Slow consumption creates deep, lasting change.

Podcasts

• **Financial Times:** ***Money Clinic***

Clear, grounded guidance on everyday money decisions.

• **The Calm Collective**

Conversations on grief, gentleness, and emotional steadiness.

• **Feel Better, Live More — Dr Rangan Chatterjee**

Holistic wellbeing, nervous-system calm, and sustainable habit change.

• **The Psychology Podcast**

Accessible insights on behaviour, identity, and why we do what we do.

Books

• **The Psychology of Money — Morgan Housel**

Timeless lessons on behaviour, simplicity, and emotional wealth.

• **Tiny Beautiful Things — Cheryl Strayed**

Compassion, humanity, and self-forgiveness in everyday life.

- **Why Has Nobody Told Me This Before? — Dr Julie Smith**

Practical emotional regulation and mindset support for real life.

- **Four Thousand Weeks — Oliver Burkeman**

A powerful reframing of time, purpose, and pace.

Choose one.

Read gently.

Let it support you, not overwhelm you.

GLOSSARY: MIDLIFE MONEY TERMS (EXPLAINED SIMPLY)

A CALM, JARGON-FREE REFERENCE FOR UK + US READERS.

A

Allowance (US)

Money you regularly give a child or teen to help them learn budgeting, saving, and spending habits.

APR (Annual Percentage Rate)

The total yearly cost of borrowing, including interest and fees. A higher APR means the debt costs you more over time.

Asset Allocation

How your investments are divided across types of assets (e.g., stocks, bonds, cash). Your mix affects both growth and fluctuation.

Automation

Letting systems move money for you so you don't rely on motivation or perfect energy. Habits that run themselves.

B

Balance Transfer (UK & US)

Moving credit card debt from one card to another, usually to benefit from a lower or 0% interest period.

Bond

A loan you give to a company or government. They pay you interest, and return your money when the bond matures.

C

Capital Gains Tax (CGT)

Tax you pay on profits from selling investments (only above allowances).

UK: Applies to most investments outside an ISA.

US: Applies to taxable brokerage accounts.

Catch-Up Contributions

Extra money you're allowed to contribute in midlife.

A gift for late starters.

You are not behind — the system literally expects late bloomers.

Compound Interest

Interest earning interest. Small amounts grow significantly over long periods.

Credit Utilisation

How much of your available credit you're using. Lower utilisation generally improves credit scores.

D

Debt Avalanche

A repayment method where you pay off the highest-interest debt first to minimise total interest paid.

Debt Snowball

A repayment method where you pay the smallest balance first for emotional momentum.

Direct Debit (UK)

An automatic payment where a company can take variable amounts from your bank account (e.g., bills or subscriptions).

Diversification

Not betting everything on one option.

Think "basket," not "egg in hand."

Dividend

A portion of a company's profits paid to shareholders.

E

Emergency Buffer

Not "three months saved immediately."

Start with £5/$5 a week.

Stability comes from habit, not heroics.

Emergency Fund

A safety pot for unexpected expenses so you don't fall into debt during tough months.

ETF (Exchange-Traded Fund)

A basket of investments you can buy like a single stock. Often low-cost and diversified.

F

Fixed Rate Mortgage

A home loan where your interest rate stays the same for a set term.

401(k): A U.S. retirement savings account often offered by employers. Contributions are pre-tax, and many employers offer matching funds.

Fund

A pool of investments managed together. Can hold hundreds or thousands of stocks or bonds.

G

GIA (General Investment Account, UK)

A standard taxable investment account with no special tax shelter, but no contribution limits.

I

Index / Index Fund

An index (e.g., S&P 500, FTSE 100) tracks a group of companies.

An index fund invests in that group automatically — simple, low-cost, long-term.

The tortoise of investing. And the tortoise wins.

Inflation

Prices rising over time. Inflation reduces the spending power of your money.

Interest Rate

The cost of borrowing or the reward for saving, shown as a percentage.

ISA (Individual Savings Account, UK)

A tax-free account where your savings or investments can grow without income or capital gains tax.

IRA (Individual Retirement Account, US)

A personal retirement account with tax advantages (Traditional or Roth).

L

Life Expectancy

An estimate of how long the average person is likely to live. Useful when planning retirement timelines.

Lifetime ISA (UK)

A savings or investment ISA where the government adds a 25% bonus for first-home buying or retirement (within limits).

M

Minimum Payment

The smallest amount you must pay toward your credit card each month to avoid late fees.

Mutual Fund

A professionally managed fund that pools money from many investors. Similar to an ETF but priced differently.

N

Net Worth

Everything you own minus everything you owe.

No moral score.

Just a picture — like a weather report.

P

Pension / Retirement Fund

Your future income pot.

UK: Pensions + State Pension.

US: 401(k), IRA, Roth IRA.

Your long-term safety net.

Pension (UK)

A retirement savings account that offers tax benefits. Includes workplace pensions and SIPPs.

Portfolio

All your investments combined — your "money garden."

Prosperisms™

Short, memorable lines throughout this book designed to anchor your mindset and support your Slow Money Reset.

R

Risk Tolerance

Your emotional comfort with the ups and downs of investing.

Yours is allowed to be gentler in midlife.

Roth IRA (US)

A retirement account where you contribute after-tax money and withdraw tax-free later.

S

S&P 500 (US)

An index of 500 large US companies. A common benchmark for long-term investing.

Salary Sacrifice (UK)

An arrangement where part of your salary goes directly into your pension before tax, reducing taxable income.

Sinking Fund

Savings pots for predictable future expenses (car repairs, holidays, home maintenance, joy purchases).

SIPP (Self-Invested Personal Pension, UK)

A type of pension where you choose your own investments.

Slow Money Movement™

A grounded, nervous-system-safe approach to building financial stability and wealth without panic, shame, or hustle.

Snowball Plus™ (Mel G Prosper)

A hybrid, trauma-aware debt repayment method combining emotional wins, financial logic, and nervous-system-safe pacing.

Unique to The Slow Money Movement™.

Stocks

Shares of ownership in a company. Over time, they usually grow more than most other asset types.

Stocks & Shares ISA (UK)

An ISA allowing you to invest in funds, ETFs, and shares with no tax on profits.

Sustainable Withdrawal Rate

A guideline for how much you can safely withdraw from investments in retirement without running out of money.

T

Tax-Deferred (US)

Money grows without being taxed until you withdraw it (e.g. Traditional IRA, 401(k)).

Tracker Fund

Another name for an index fund — it "tracks" a specific market.

W

Will

A legal document stating who receives your assets and who handles your affairs after death.

Withdrawal Rate

How much of your savings or investments you take out each year in retirement.

Workplace Pension (UK)

A pension arranged by your employer, usually with employer contributions.

YOUR SECOND-ACT WEALTH PLEDGE

I do not rush.
I do not compare.
I do not shrink from numbers or from life.
I build what I can, when I can, with what I have.
I protect my nervous system.
I protect my peace.
I protect my future self.
I am not catching up.
I am growing up — financially, emotionally, and intentionally.
Slow is not stuck.
Slow is mastery.
Slow is wealth.
I am building a life I can live inside.
And I am doing it with grace.
Signature: ______________________________
Date: __________________________________

END NOTE TO THE READER

I didn't write this book to impress anyone with a perfect financial system.

I wrote it because I know what it feels like to rebuild — while juggling responsibilities, exhaustion, work, worry, and the quiet pressure to be "sorted" by now.

I wrote it because midlife deserves a different kind of financial guidance — one that honours bandwidth, bodies, and real lives.

If you take only one thing from these pages, let it be this:

Your pace is allowed.

Your clarity is enough.

Your future is still open.

The Slow Money philosophy isn't about becoming wealthy overnight.

It's about becoming well enough to create a life that holds you. A life that feels like an exhale instead of a performance.

Thank you for letting me walk beside you.

It has been a privilege.

— *Mel G Prosper*

ACKNOWLEDGMENTS

To everyone who has ever felt behind, afraid, late, tired, embarrassed, or quietly determined to begin again — this book is for you.

To those who rebuilt quietly, who chose peace when the world shouted urgency, who protected their energy, and who took small steps while carrying heavy burdens — I see you. You are proof that slow strength is still strength.

To the readers balancing ageing parents and grown children, mortgages and hormones, grief and hope, fatigue and ambition — you are the backbone of families and the unsung stabilisers of society. May this book be a hand on your back, not a weight on your shoulders.

To the midlife starters, restart-ers, late bloomers, survivors, and soft fighters — thank you for letting me walk beside you.

To my family and friends — your love and support sit quietly under every page.

To my community — seen and unseen — who encouraged me to bring Slow Money into the world… thank you for trusting that gentleness is not weakness, and that sustainable wealth is emotional work as much as numbers.

And to my younger and future selves — thank you for holding each other across time. We got here slowly. And that is the point.

ABOUT THE AUTHOR

Mel G. Prosper is a writer, slow-wealth advocate, and compassionate guide for midlife reinvention. After navigating financial anxiety, burnout, caregiving responsibilities, and the quiet courage required to rebuild in midlife, Mel founded the **Slow Money Movement™** — a philosophy grounded in emotional safety, sustainable wealth, and nervous-system-friendly financial growth.

Mel believes wealth isn't speed.

It's stability.

It's dignity.

It's choice.

It's breathing room.

It's agency.

It's a future that feels safe to step into.

Through a blend of behavioural finance, midlife psychology, and calm-wealth principles, Mel helps readers create lives they can actually live inside — slowly, steadily, and without shame.

Discover more calm-money tools and resources at:

SlowMoneyMovement.com

DISCLAIMER

This book is intended for informational, educational, and personal reflection purposes only. It does not constitute financial, legal, medical, psychological, or therapeutic advice.

The author is not acting as a financial adviser, accountant, therapist, clinician, or legal professional. All concepts relating to budgeting, investing, earning, saving, debt strategies, emotional frameworks, and behavioural tools are provided for general educational use within the Slow Money Movement™ philosophy.

Readers should consult a qualified professional before making decisions regarding:

- personal finances
- pensions or retirement planning
- taxation
- investments
- debt management
- legal documents (wills, power of attorney, etc.)
- medical concerns
- mental health or emotional wellbeing

Every financial and life situation is unique. Examples, stories, and case studies included in this book are illustrative only and do not guarantee any specific outcomes. Past results or experiences described do not predict future results.

Published by **The Reset Edit Ltd**

www.ingramcontent.com/pod-product-compliance
Lightning Source LLC
LaVergne TN
LVHW101615210926
848480LV00010B/1448